THE
MIDEAST PEACE
PROCESS

$30
(415)

THE
MIDEAST PEACE
PROCESS
AN AUTOPSY

EDITED BY **NEAL KOZODOY**

ENCOUNTER BOOKS
SAN FRANCISCO, CALIFORNIA

Paperback published in 2002 by Encounter Books, an activity of Encounter for Culture and Education, Inc., a nonprofit tax exempt corporation.

Encounter Books website address: www.encounterbooks.com

Manufactured in the United States and printed on acid-free paper.

The paper used in this publication meets the minimum requirements of ANSI/NISO Z39.48-1992 (R 1997)(*Permanence of Paper*).

Library of Congress Cataloging-in-Publication Data

Available upon request.

10 9 8 7 6 5

Contents

Preface

Only the principals knew for sure, on that September day in 1993, how the world-historical agreement being signed in brilliant sunlight on the lawn of the White House, and sealed with a handshake before an assemblage of transfixed dignitaries and guests, was even then in the process of being subverted—had already been subverted.

At the signing ceremony, one party, Israel—through its prime minister, Yitzhak Rabin, and its foreign minister, Shimon Peres—was formally recognizing the Palestine Liberation Organization (PLO) as the representative of the Palestinian people and committing itself to the peaceful resolution of their differences. The other party, the PLO, having (in the days leading up to this moment) silently withdrawn its previous undertakings to Israeli negotiators, was still not agreeing to declare an end to armed struggle, or even to set a date for renouncing its official aim of destroying the Jewish state. To the contrary, on the day of the signing itself, Yasir Arafat, the chairman of the PLO, would broadcast to the Palestinian people in Arabic that the peace accord to which he had affixed his name was nothing more than a first step in a longstanding plan for the "phased" elimination of Israel.

So, in deception and self-deception, began the Middle East "peace process," a chain of events that would emerge as the first if not the costliest folly of the post-cold-war age. Among the questions likely to engage future historians contemplating this folly, a good number will surely concern what may or may not have been in the minds of Israeli negotiators and politicians who had to be aware of the nature of the partner with whom they were dealing and the activity in which they were engaged, and yet, averting their faces and the world's from what they knew, plunged ahead anyway. Questions such as these:

When it entered into secret negotiations at Oslo and then into its "partnership" with the PLO, a radical terrorist group just then at the nadir of its own political fortunes, was Israel being unwillingly dragged by developments, either in its region or internationally, which it felt it had no choice but to accommodate? Conversely, did it perceive itself, in the aftermath of the collapse of the Soviet Union and the defeat of Iraq in the Gulf war, to be in a unique and possibly ephemeral position of regional strength, a position enabling it, at a stroke, to preempt and subdue one threat to its security while at the same time creating a buffer between itself and other, still larger ones? To what degree may it have been motivated by feelings of historic guilt vis-à-vis the Palestinian Arabs in the territories it had controlled since the Six-Day war of June 1967? What role was played, after more than four decades of armed conflict, by simple weariness; or by "post-Zionist" aspirations toward a society rid of the burdens, physical and moral, of an occupying power; or by sheer utopianism?

Most troublesome of all, how could any, or even all, of these considerations have sufficed to induce Israel to throw to the winds its decades-old strategy of deterrent strength and embrace as its "peace partner" the most implacable and ambitious of its enemies? How could it then have proceeded to bring this enemy home from exile, to rehabilitate its sunken international credit, invest it with political authority, help to equip it with arms and money, acquiesce in its indoctrination of young Palestinians in the hatred and killing of Jews, suffer its every resort to violence, whitewash its every lie?

We need not, as it happens, wait very long for such questions to be asked. In the fiery months after the implosion of the Oslo peace process in September 2000, no one would pose them more plaintively, or bitterly, than hundreds of thousands of crushed Israelis, including some who had been Oslo's most ardent champions within the country's political and cultural establishments. Indeed, a new question would quickly be added to the list: why, even after the deceptions and self-deceptions of Oslo had at last been unmasked and reality could no longer be denied, were voices still to be heard insisting with grotesque inconsequence that, in the words of the then-departing American ambassador to Israel, "just because the Middle East peace process failed does not mean it should be abandoned"?

To answer these questions adequately will no doubt require whole dissertations in politics and psychology. But in any survey of relevant factors, what should not be overlooked is the volume of sustaining *applause* that was generated worldwide by the news of the Oslo accords, amplified a hundredfold at the September 1993 ceremony on the White House lawn and then supplemented with equal parts of international and, especially, American cajolery and blandishment as year to year the process wended its tortuous way, from declarations of brotherly intent to violation after violation by the PLO to concession after concession by Israel to renewed acts of Palestinian violence and so forth in dismal progression.

Yet through all this, and no matter how brutal the serial effects, not least on those Palestinians who had been relegated to life under Yasir Arafat's regime, the peace process never lost its aura of sanctified approval among the West's enlightened classes. In the print media and on the air, in churches and synagogues, in universities and diplomatic circles, in foundations and international forums, the rightness of the enterprise lay stubbornly beyond question. This consensus became, in itself, a chief weapon in the hands of Oslo's backers and apologists, wielded with effectiveness to silence any who might raise a doubt as to its origins, its course, or its likely consequences. For who, after all, could be against "peace"?

· · · · ·

That is where this book comes in. The essays in it have been selected out of a much larger number on the subject that were published in *Commentary* magazine over the course of the Oslo years. By presenting them chronologically, in the order in which they appeared, we hope to give some sense of the way in which the peace process itself developed, and of its shifting nuances and priorities. But since the very first such article there could certainly be no mistaking the magazine's general perspective. In stark contrast to almost every editorialist and columnist and political observer who thought and wrote about the Oslo peace process, the magazine's authors not only failed to applaud or endorse it, but took a deeply skeptical view: skeptical of Oslo's origins, its course, and its likely consequences.

They were not afraid that Oslo might succeed in bringing peace. They saw that it rested on a deep misreading of the true disposition of the Arab side, and that its implementation could not allay but rather only inflame extremist passions among Palestinians, not enhance but

worsen Israel's physical security, not mitigate but excite the Arab determination to achieve the eventual destruction of the Jewish state. In short,
they were afraid it was calculated to end in disaster, to bring not peace
but war. So indeed it gives every indication of having done.

That the dissenting position taken by *Commentary*'s writers should,
at the time, have been quite so isolated as it was—and so harshly attacked
and condemned—is itself a pertinent fact, redolent of the atmosphere of
willed, illusory expectation, coupled with moral bullying, in which the
peace process was manufactured and sold. Now that Oslo's moment has
passed and the human price of its folly is being paid, and paid again,
these essays can perhaps be appreciated at their truer worth: as astute
and remarkably prescient exercises in contemporary historical analysis.
Case studies of a temptation to which democratic societies of all kinds
and places have been peculiarly susceptible, may they also serve, however fleetingly, as a warning in the face of similar temptations to come.

David Bar-Illan

Israel's
New Pollyannas

Until recently, it was not difficult to define the main obstacle to a peace agreement between Arabs and Israelis: the very minimum the Syrians and Palestinians could accept exceeded the maximum Israel could give.

In practical terms, this meant that since Hafez al-Assad's Syria could accept no less than what Anwar Sadat's Egypt had received—every inch of land lost to the Israelis in war—and since Israel could not afford to relinquish all this land (which would bring the border to within yards of the Sea of Galilee), an agreement with Syria was impossible.

Similarly, no Palestinian leader could accept anything less than total Israeli withdrawal to the 1949 armistice lines (usually described as the 1967 borders—that is, the borders until the Six-Day war in June of that year) and the establishment of a Palestinian state with the eastern half of Jerusalem as its capital, while no Israeli government could allow this to happen. Ergo, the prospects of a Palestinian-Israeli agreement were nonexistent.

All the procedural arguments—for instance, the Arabs' insistence on an international conference to decide the issue rather than direct talks between the parties—were merely a function of these differences. The Arabs, correctly assuming that Israel—no matter who was in the government—would not deliver their minimal demands, saw in a UN-sponsored conference a venue in which the world tribunal would impose an unpalatable settlement on Israel.

1

That is why the Madrid conference of 1991 was considered a small miracle. Israel, Jordan, Lebanon, Syria, and the Palestinians actually sat down to negotiate in bilateral, direct talks. This, despite the fact that the then-Israeli government was a hawkish Likud-led coalition, headed by the stubborn Yitzhak Shamir, and that to expect it to bend to Palestinian demands for sovereignty in Judea, Samaria, and Gaza, or to accept Syrian claims to all of the Golan Heights, was ludicrous.

But the meeting took place at least partly because it was conceived in deception. In secret private letters, the Bush administration was able to convince each participant that the U.S. would support its position. Thus, Syria was promised not only that the American (and Soviet) sponsors of the talks would play an important mediating role when it mattered, but that Washington saw "the return of territories according to UN Resolutions 242 and 338"—a formula which to the Arabs translated into total withdrawal—as applicable to the Golan.

Similarly, the U.S. assured the Palestinians that it was still committed to the general outline of the Rogers plan of 1969, which called for virtually complete Israeli withdrawal to the 1949 armistice lines, and that it considered the Israeli annexation of the eastern part of Jerusalem illegal. In the eyes of the U.S., the Palestinians were reminded, east Jerusalem was still "occupied territory." (As it happens, even west Jerusalem has not been recognized by the U.S. as part of Israel.) The message was unmistakable: the U.S. would support the establishment of a Palestinian homeland in the territories with east Jerusalem as its capital. Indeed, for the first time since 1967, an American administration refused Israel's request to say that it actively opposed a Palestinian state.

To assuage Israel's fears of American support for a Palestinian state, however, the Bush administration did specifically agree to exclude the PLO from the negotiating process, and to insist on a joint Jordanian-Palestinian delegation, thus eliminating any semblance of a separate, independent Palestinian entity. Israel also received a commitment that only inhabitants of the territories could become delegates to the talks. That is, neither residents of Jerusalem nor members of the Palestinian "diaspora" would be eligible.

Furthermore, Israel was assured that the U.S. stood by President Gerald Ford's commitment to "give weight" to Israel's security concerns in the Golan Heights, that the Jerusalem question would be raised only at a later stage of the negotiations, and that the negotiations would be based on the formula worked out at Camp David in the 1978 talks leading up to the breakthrough agreement between Israel and Egypt. This last meant an interim period of Palestinian autonomy for five years, with negotiations for a permanent solution beginning after the third year. All options would be left open—including the possibility of an Israeli demand for sovereignty over the territories.

· · · · ·

These assurances to the various parties were clearly irreconcilable. Charitably, they were white lies intended to get everyone together in the hope that differences would be ironed out at the negotiating table. A more cynical interpretation would characterize them as a stratagem designed to create an irresistible momentum which would force Israel to yield to the prevailing world demand for total withdrawal. Either way, then-Prime Minister Yitzhak Shamir did not appreciate their import. When asked about the American assurances to the Arabs, he said Israel was not bound by American promises. All that mattered was that the talks were bilateral and direct, and that the U.S. would not interfere.

But conflicting promises have a way of exploding. On the very first day of the Madrid conference, the Palestinian representatives, who were supposed to be included in the Jordanian delegation, were allotted the same space at the table as the other delegations and allowed a separate time slot for their addresses. Armed with American support for them as a distinct delegation, they stalled the negotiations for months until the Israelis yielded. Washington also allowed Faisal Husseini, a resident of Jerusalem and a member of Yasir Arafat's Fatah organization—and therefore doubly ineligible for participation—to head an "advisory team" attached to the delegation. He and the team's spokeswoman, Hanan Ashrawi, promptly became the most sought-after stars of the peace talks. The Jordanian delegation faded into the background.

In addition, the Bush administration circumvented the ban on the PLO by letting senior PLO figures enter the U.S. for post-Madrid negotiations in Washington. Setting up shop in the delegates' hotel, they were ostentatiously consulted by the official Palestinian participants before and after every session. The commitment to exclude "diaspora" Palestinians was also broken, when Mohammad Khalaj, a member of the Palestine National Council who lives in America, was included in the negotiations on refugees at the multilateral talks on regional problems. And the final obliteration of the American commitment to exclude the PLO and Jerusalem residents came when Israel (now led by Yitzhak Rabin) agreed, as part of the deal with the U.S. (now led by Bill Clinton) following the expulsion of 400 Hamas agitators, to the formal recognition of Husseini as head of the Palestinian delegation.*

· · · · ·

But far more disturbing than the American manipulations were those practiced by the Israeli government itself. For some three years, the Syrians had been spreading the word that Assad had had a change of heart. Having lost the sponsorship of the Soviets, he purportedly now realized that he would never achieve strategic parity with Israel—a euphemism for a military capability which would enable him to vanquish Israel on his own. Forced to get closer to the West to survive, and aware that the West wanted peace, he was ready to sign an agreement with Israel.

This line was startlingly similar to the argument made in 1990 by Saddam Hussein and *his* supporters in the West and in Israel. (Among those convinced at the time that Saddam was so eager to curry favor with the West that he would be a natural candidate for a peace treaty with Israel was Ezer Weizman, now Israel's President.) That Saddam himself proved the fallacy of the argument—he not only betrayed his promises but started a war in the Gulf without Soviet backing—seemed to be forgotten.

President Hosni Mubarak of Egypt, who weeks before Iraq's invasion of Kuwait had assured Israel of Saddam's benignity, was credited both with persuading Assad of the advantages of peace and with convincing the U.S. that the Syrian dictator was sincere. As Egypt had discovered in the late 1970s, lost land (in Egypt's case, the Sinai peninsula) could be retrieved from Israel more easily through peace than by war. And Assad, a reputed pragmatist who had repeatedly vowed to destroy Israel if it took 200 years, now saw that sitting with Israel at the negotiating table made sense. True, to mitigate an implied recognition of the Jewish state, the Syrians insisted on calling the negotiations an international conference, but in reality they agreed to participate in strictly bilateral talks.

The Syrians at first found the role of peace partners a little unnatural. But eager to get their country off the State Department list of states

---

*Predictably, this made the Palestinians assume they could bring up the matter of Jerusalem immediately, rather than at the negotiations on the permanent solution. This in turn caused an impasse in the negotiations which prompted the Clinton administration to send a diplomatic team headed by Dennis Ross to Israel to reconcile PLO and Israeli positions.

that sponsored terrorism, they even chimed in with a confidence-building measure, allowing the gradual emigration of Syrian Jews provided they did not go to Israel. And as soon as the Israeli delegation, under the Labor government, announced Israel's readiness to withdraw from the Golan Heights, they switched from displays of cold fury to smiles and handshakes. These prompted the new Israeli Foreign Minister, Shimon Peres, to proclaim that the developments in Damascus were nothing short of sensational.

What the Syrians made clear, however, was that they expected the negotiations to bring nothing less than full Israeli withdrawal not only from the Golan Heights—small in area but strategically vital for the defense of Israel's north—but from all areas occupied by Israel in 1967 and 1982. This meant the complete evacuation of Judea, Samaria, Gaza, east Jerusalem, and Israel's security belt in southern Lebanon.

Nor was Syria willing to sign a full-fledged peace treaty in return. It interpreted UN Resolution 242 to mean that Israel must withdraw from *all* captured territory on *all* fronts (a transparently false reading), and that in return Israel was entitled to nothing more than an end to the state of belligerency that would not include a peace treaty and normalization of relations.

Though aware of the Syrian position, Rabin—who a day before the Israeli election had said that anyone abandoning the Golan Heights would be guilty of forsaking Israel's security—predicted that "within months" Israel and Syria would sign on the dotted line. Members of the cabinet, including Police Minister Moshe Shahal who was known for his closeness to Rabin, openly advocated relinquishing the entire Golan.

To be sure, Rabin himself kept stressing that he would consider withdrawing only *on* the Golan Heights, not *from* them. But he kept all options open by allowing that the extent of withdrawal depended on the quality of peace Syria was prepared to offer. This was generally understood to mean that for a full-fledged peace treaty, which would include an exchange of ambassadors and a free flow of people and goods between the two countries, Rabin would forfeit Israeli sovereignty in the Golan and effect a gradual but complete withdrawal. In that case, leaks from government offices averred, to ensure against Syrian aggression, Rabin would insist that the area be demilitarized and the U.S. station troops between Syrians and Israelis.

Rabin's "you tell me first what kind of peace you want and I'll tell you how much land I'll give" created the impression that the Syrians had not made their position clear. Yet soon after the resumption of negotiations under the Labor government, the Syrian delegation submitted a document summarizing its position. It indicated that Damascus had not budged an inch from its insistence on total Israeli withdrawal to the 1949 armistice lines on all fronts, and that in return it was willing to commit to no more than a state of nonbelligerency.

This document so disappointed the Israeli government that it asked the Syrian delegation not to publish it, a request that may have constituted a historic first: a democratic government asking a dictatorial regime to keep an exchange secret for fear that the information would adversely affect public opinion. To this day, the only open source of the document's contents is the Arab press to which it was leaked by the Syrians. Israel has yet to release it.

. . . . .

This, however, was a relatively minor episode in a much more elaborate effort by the Israeli government—one in which the press collaborated—to sell Assad not only as a leader who needed and wanted peace but as a man of honor. The evidence for this, said ministers and columnists, was there for all to see: the 1974 separation agreement on the Golan Heights, which had been observed by Syria for twenty years (with the exception of a few forays by terrorists, for which the Syrians were not held responsible). Assad might be a ruthless dictator, but his signature on a contract would be binding.

Forgotten were a few pertinent facts. The reason the Syrians have been careful not to provoke the Israelis on the Golan Heights is that the Israeli army there is within striking distance of Damascus. In Lebanon, where Israeli retaliation can hurt only Hezbollah cadres, Palestinian terrorists, and Shiite villagers, Syria's scruples about agreements have seemed to disappear.

Indeed, Assad's record of broken agreements easily matches that of other Middle Eastern dictators. In 1983, he broke a pledge he had made to the Reagan administration (via the Saudis) that he would accept the Israeli-Lebanese peace treaty and withdraw his troops from Lebanon. He did the opposite: as soon as Israel began to get out, he poured more troops into Lebanon. He completed the effective annexation of the country in 1990, after having joined the anti-Iraq coalition and being rewarded by the Bush administration with carte blanche in Beirut. And recently his Foreign Minister, Farouk al-Sharaa, declared that Lebanon and Syria were "like one country."

Assad is also in violation of the Saudi-sponsored Taif agreement, endorsed by all the Arab states, which stipulates the withdrawal of Syrian troops and the restoration of Lebanese. sovereignty. September 1993 marks precisely a year since Syrian troops were supposed to have left Beirut.

Even more puzzling is the current Israeli government's support of the notion—a favorite of European and American diplomats—that Assad is pursuing peace. Hezbollah, the Iranian-financed organization whose almost daily attacks on Israeli targets finally led to the retaliatory strikes of late July, trains its 3,000–5,000 highly motivated fighters in Syrian camps, under Syrian supervision, in Lebanon's Bekaa valley. It is equipped with Syrian arms, including potent Sager missiles, and Iranian arms brought through Damascus. The organization could not have mounted a single major operation against Israel without Syrian approval. Yet as soon as Labor came to power, Hezbollah became an "Iranian organization" operating independently. Indeed, it was only after the cease-fire ending the fighting in late July that Syria's role in "standing behind" Hezbollah was alluded to by Rabin (which did not prevent him from praising Assad a few days later).

Ignored, too, has been Syrian sponsorship of the Palestinians who openly call for the destruction of the Jewish state by force of arms. Last year, Syria held a conference of the ten "rejectionist" groups—among them Hamas, Islamic Jihad, and the radical PLO factions—in Damascus, where many of these organizations have their headquarters. Syria also directs the operation of Radio Al Quds, beamed to the administered territories, which incites Palestinians against the "traitors" in their midst who negotiate with Israel. Unlike their Israeli apologists, the Syrians are quite frank about supporting the "armed struggle" as long as Israel occupies "Arab land." And they have flatly rejected Israeli demands to disarm Hezbollah and the Palestinians in southern Lebanon. In the peace talks the Syrians have rejected all Israeli suggestions to discuss a truce in Lebanon.

Nor has Assad slowed down the feverish pace of Syrian arming. Having replenished and modernized all branches of its armed forces, Syria surpasses Israel in virtually all major classes of military equipment, let alone in the number of troops. In April, Syria began to manufacture Scud-C missiles in factories near Hama and Aleppo.

Occasionally, Prime Minister Rabin and Foreign Minister Peres mention Syrian missile acquisitions and continued Syrian testing of sophisticated missiles. Israeli field commanders on the northern front also talk gravely of Syria's formidable new power. But mostly government spokesmen suggest that the Assad regime's march to peace is inexorable and must not be interrupted with irritating cavils about arms build-ups or backing Hezbollah.

The press is even worse. Not unlike Soviet apologists in the West during the cold war, Assad's promoters in the Israeli media explain that Syria is just as concerned about an Israeli attack as Israel is about Syrian aggression. Only when ambushes and shelling by Hezbollah cost the lives of Israeli soldiers in July did the press begin to question Syria's role, gingerly. Yet after the mini-Lebanese war caused by these attacks, Syria was given credit for helping to end it.

The army brass, too, has collaborated in pushing the notion that an agreement with Syria is a *sine qua non* of peace. The chief of the General Staff, Ehud Barak, making the kind of political pronouncement men in uniform are usually expected to avoid, has warned that failure to achieve an agreement with Syria would trigger a countdown to war. To which one wag responded, "Does such a countdown mean that Syria would start arming?" Barak also extolled Assad as a "responsible leader" following the cease-fire in Lebanon.

A similar make-believe approach has dominated the government line on the Palestinians. Terrorist attacks on Israelis are routinely attributed either to lone Muslim fanatics suddenly driven to murder Jews, or to the actions of Hamas cells. Yet the truth is that a majority of terrorist acts, against both Jews and Palestinian Arabs accused of "collaboration," are committed by the secular Fatah, Arafat's own group in the PLO. And despite the reputed rivalry between the PLO and Hamas, some of the operations are mounted by them as joint efforts. Arafat himself has repeatedly taken credit for every "execution" in the territories. ("I approve every file," he once said, "if not before the execution, then after it.")

Nevertheless, government spokesmen prefer to pretend that the killers are not operatives of the "moderate" Arafat, supporter of the peace talks, but "enemies of the peace process" such as Hamas, Islamic Jihad, and PLO radicals like the Habash, Hawatmeh, and Jibril groups. The not unreasonable assumption behind this charade is that the public might resent continued talks with proxies of the "mainstream" PLO in Washington while its gunmen are killing Israelis back home.

The separation between negotiators and killers was reinforced by Peres when he was asked why the subject of continued terrorism, both in Israel and the administered territories as well as on the Lebanon border, was not brought up at the peace talks. "Because the people who are doing the talking are not the people who are doing the shooting," he answered.

Yet leaving aside whether it makes sense to negotiate with people who do not control those "who are doing the shooting," the government is perfectly aware of Arafat's connection with terrorist activity. In early July, Minister of Health Haim Ramon, a rising Labor-party star who often represents the government in Knesset debates, was reported to have contacted Arafat with the proposal of a trade: direct Israeli negotiations with the PLO in exchange for the cessation of terrorism. The answer was a flat no.

This points to another government-propagated myth. When asked about the absence of reciprocal gestures by the Palestinians, Peres said, "There is nothing the Palestinians could give us. We just have to decide what we want to give them." In fact, however, a halt to terrorism is only one "confidence-building" gesture the Palestinians might make. Another would be to lift the boycott on Israeli goods in the territories and to appeal to the Arab states to terminate their economic boycott against Israel. But the Palestinians have been doing the exact opposite. When Kuwait announced that it was lifting the "secondary" boycott—the banning of foreign companies that do business with Israel from Arab markets—the Palestinian leadership yelled treason.

What Israel's government seems unwilling to admit, perhaps even to itself, is that terrorist activity and guerrilla warfare are not "a campaign against the peace process." Individual members of groups like Hamas and Hezbollah may indeed believe that the peace process is a satanic Zionist-American plot, but the Arabs participating in the peace negotiations who use the services of these organizations—Syria and the PLO—are simply following a traditional totalitarian strategy of shooting while talking.

The immediate purpose of the shooting is to inflict as many Israeli casualties as possible. ("I want Israel to see a funeral a day on the TV screen," Assad said during the Israeli withdrawal from Lebanon in 1984.) The ultimate goal is to create internal pressure in Israel for a speedier peace settlement that would presumably stop the killing. A grieving mother from the northern Israeli town of Kiryat Shemona was shown on television after a Katyusha bombardment from Lebanon, crying, "Enough, give them what they want, it's time to make peace." Similarly, clashes with the army are aimed at demoralizing Israel's soldiers. If peace is really at hand, getting killed defending a piece of land slated to be relinquished makes little sense.

· · · · ·

It is, of course, possible that branding the terrorists "enemies of the peace process" is the government's way of deflecting criticism from its Left flank for its tough anti-terrorist measures. After all, Rabin sold his super-dovish Meretz coalition partners on the expulsion of 400 Hamas agitators by assuring them that it would strengthen the PLO's position and help the peace process. And following this year's Black March, in which terrorist killings—mostly inside the Green Line—occurred almost daily, the government imposed an open-ended closure on the administered territories with nary a peep from Meretz. (Had a Likud government deprived 120,000 Arab workers of their livelihood for any length of time, the Left would have been in an uproar heard around the world.)

In the first weeks of the closure, terrorist attacks ceased almost completely. That Palestinian laborers were prevented from crossing the Green Line caused hardship and losses not only to them but to Israeli builders, industrialists, and farmers. Yet the public reacted with a sigh of relief. At which point the Labor government began to view the closure as more than a security measure; now it was seen as a brilliant political move. The assumption was that the luxury of life free of terrorism would make a majority of Israelis long for the day when Israel would relinquish the territories.

What seems to have been overlooked in this picture was that only the Israeli army's presence in the territories made the closure effective. Nor was this effectiveness a product of the separation in itself. Greatly assisted by the forced immobility of the population, the army could now make virtually unhindered house-to-house searches, discover terrorist cells, and round up known individual terrorists by the hundreds. The results were nothing short of spectacular. Most of the men wanted for killings of Israelis and "collaborators" were either apprehended or forced to flee the country (mainly to Egypt).

It was this blow to the terrorist organizations, rather than the closure—which was in effect suspended within weeks—that reduced terrorist activities to a minimum. But the government, preferring to attribute the relaxation to "the separation," continued to perpetuate the myth that the closure was still in effect well after 60,000 registered Palestinian workers and 10,000 others had returned to work in Israel.

The government also seems to have overlooked something else. The brief initial separation of the Palestinians in the territories from Jerusalem made *them* realize how dependent they are on their leaders and their offices, institutions, newspapers, and information services, all of which are located in the eastern part of the city. Ultimately, the most dramatic accomplishment of the closure may have been the sharpening of the Palestinian demand for the inclusion of east Jerusalem in the autonomy plan and the future Palestinian state. "The Israelis and the Americans had better realize," said the Palestinian negotiator Haidar Abdel Shafi in mid-July, "that without an Arab Jerusalem there will be no peace."

Shafi's observation is probably correct. His assessment of the ten rounds of talks in the twenty months since Madrid as utterly devoid of results is also far more accurate than Peres's glowing expressions of optimism. (Rabin has been more restrained.) Even the agreement with Jordan—"all we need is a pen to sign it with," said Peres before the beginning of the tenth round—proved a chimera. The delegations had come together on a draft according to which Israel would relinquish areas on the Jordan river bank and south of the Dead Sea, in return for Jordan's willingness to sign an agenda containing the words, "it is anticipated that the process will culminate in a peace treaty." But the draft, subject to approval by the respective governments, came back from Amman with "minor clarifications": the Jerusalem issue must be resolved first; all the administered territories must be referred to as "occupied"; and the reference to a peace treaty at the end of the road must be eliminated. Here, too, the negotiations were back to square one.

· · · · ·

The Labor government's negotiating strategy is not easy to fathom. From the start, Rabin made one concession after another without a hint of reciprocation. Before the tenth post-Madrid round he declared—implicitly acknowledging what he had been doing up to that point—that the time of one-sided concessions was over. But he never said what he expected from the Arab side.

Concomitantly, the government has been portraying developments in rosy terms when in fact no progress has been registered. Even the one concession the Syrians had made to the Likud government of Yitzhak Shamir—allowing Syrian Jews to emigrate—was withdrawn soon after Labor came to power in early 1992. Nor did the hoped-for moderation of Palestinian demands—which was supposed to follow Israel's agreement to include Jerusalemite Faisal Husseini in the Palestinian delegation—ever materialize. On the contrary, the question of Jerusalem, which must be postponed to a later stage if any progress is to be made on the interim arrangements, became the central issue.

Overly optimistic pronouncements are probably unavoidable during negotiations. They are often used to create momentum and place the ball in the adversary's court. But under present circumstances it is difficult to see the purpose of a consistently Pollyanna-ish Israeli campaign. One possible explanation is that the government is deceiving itself about the willingness of the Arabs to make peace on terms that do not entail full Israeli withdrawal from the Golan Heights, as well as all other territories taken in the Six-Day war, and a Palestinian state with east Jerusalem as its capital. Another, less charitable, explanation is that the dovish faction led by Peres hopes to make the expectation of peace so overwhelming that prices that seemed prohibitive to the Israeli people only yesterday will seem worth paying tomorrow.

The Palestinians, like all the Arab regimes, enjoy an advantage democracies do not have. They can be intransigent and hard-nosed without fear of internal pressures for concessions and compromises. On the contrary, they must fear assassination if they *do* make concessions. Whatever some Israeli doves may imagine, it is a given that the Palestinians will not budge from the demand that autonomy—and later sovereignty—include half of Jerusalem. And it can be taken for granted that they will not agree to any substantial compromises on the territorial definition of autonomy: it will have to extend to all of Judea, Samaria, and Gaza. Nor will they give up on officially including the PLO in the talks.

Against these demands stands Yitzhak Rabin, who still insists on a few traditional Labor-party "no's": no discussion of the permanent solution before autonomy is established; no return to the 1949 armistice lines; no relinquishing of the Jordan valley and Gush Etzion settlements; no direct negotiations with the PLO; and no compromise on Jerusalem, which must stay undivided under Israeli sovereignty. But Deputy Foreign Minister Yossi Beilin, who voices Peres's opinions, has indicated a willingness to yield on *all* these points—with the possible exception of Jerusalem.

If Peres, Beilin, and the dovish faction in the government have their way, the gap between the Arabs' minimum and Israel's maximum will become so narrow as to be imperceptible. And what until recently was quite unthinkable—the establishment of a Palestinian state in the administered territories, the relinquishment of the Golan Heights, and perhaps even the division of Jerusalem into two capitals—may become official government policy.

—September 1993

Yigal Carmon

The Story Behind the Handshake

The August 1993 agreement reached in Oslo between Israel and the PLO, and then signed (with some modifications) on the White House lawn a month later, was negotiated in the deepest secrecy. So far, the story behind it has been told only selectively and only by participants or supporters who see it as a triumphant historical breakthrough. But a very different picture emerges when that story is told more fully.

Oslo was by no means the first place in which PLO officials had met with Israelis. From the 1970s on, symposia, conferences, and "dialogues," open as well as clandestine, were held in cities throughout the world under various organizational, semiofficial, and even UN auspices, usually with the host countries' participation. As time went on, the Israeli participants became bolder, notwithstanding the Israeli law which prohibited direct unauthorized contact with members of the PLO. (This law was repealed shortly after the Labor party came to power in 1992.)

The Scandinavian countries had always seemed particularly eager to play the role of host in encounters between the PLO, an organization whose cause they had consistently espoused, and Israeli "peace activists" or dovish American Jews. It was in Stockholm that a group of such Americans, including Rita Hauser and Menachem Rosensaft, met with Yasir Arafat in 1988, clearing a path to the dialogue with the PLO that was begun in the last days of the Reagan administration.

That dialogue was suspended when Arafat refused to condemn a May 1990 terrorist attack on a beach near Tel Aviv by one of the mainstream PLO factions. Washington was particularly miffed when it discovered that the group had intended to attack not only Israelis, but also the American embassy. However, Arafat's refusal to dissociate himself from Abu Abbas, the group's leader, did not have the same effect on the Israeli "peace camp" as it did on the U.S. government. Israeli doves continued to meet with the PLO throughout the world, with at least one major colloquy made into an hour-long program that was widely distributed by PBS.

Among the various hosts of these meetings, a think tank called FAFO (the Norwegian acronym for Institute for Applied Social Science) was outstanding in its dedication and zeal. Early in the summer of 1992, its executive director, Terje Rod Larsen, sought out Yossi Beilin, then head of the Israeli research institute ECF (Economic Cooperation Foundation), and a protégé and very close confidant of Shimon Peres, one of the main leaders of the Labor party. Larsen told Beilin that the Palestinians were tired of the *intifada,* the campaign of violence that had been launched against Israel in 1987, and were ready to reach an agreement. If the coming election brought Labor to power, the opportunity should not be missed. Beilin responded by putting Larsen in touch with a friend, Professor Yair Hirschfeld of Haifa University, a fan of the late Austrian Chancellor Bruno Kreisky, who was famous for his Pollyanna-ish notions about the Arab-Israeli conflict.

Following the Labor victory in early 1992, Yitzhak Rabin became Prime Minister, Shimon Peres became Foreign Minister, and Peres appointed Beilin as his deputy. Larsen—whose wife was administrative assistant to the Norwegian Foreign Minister, Johan Jorgen Holst, while Holst's own wife was the FAFO chairman—now offered the services of the Norwegian government to Beilin. Holst himself was known to be "possessed" by the idea of making peace between Israel and the PLO. There could be no cozier arrangement.

Beilin could not officially participate in direct contacts with PLO representatives—they were still illegal—but he assured Larsen that Hirschfeld and a former student of his, Ron Pundik, an academic with a Scandinavian background, could do the job. At the time, says Beilin, he considered the encounter no more than an intellectual exercise.

Nor did the PLO take the Hirschfeld-Pundik pair too seriously— not until Hanan Ashrawi, the PLO spokeswoman whose home they used to visit, realized how close they were to Shimon Peres's new deputy and closest confidant. At that point, Ashrawi arranged for them to see the PLO's "Finance Minister" Abu Ala in London, and it was there that the idea of drafting a proposal for an Israel-PLO agreement was formed.

Hirschfeld suggested that meetings continue in Oslo, and the PLO people concurred.

Pundik and Hirschfeld kept stressing to their PLO counterparts that the Israeli government might disavow them at any moment. But this only served to convince the Palestinians that their Israeli interlocutors were indeed representing the government. In fact, however, virtually no one in Israel knew of the talks. Hirschfeld and Pundik's only contact at the time was with Beilin, and it is not quite clear at what stage Beilin reported their dealings to Peres.

What *is* certain is that Prime Minister Yitzhak Rabin was entirely unaware of these developments, at least until December 1992, when the Oslo negotiators came up with a document which was, according to Beilin, essentially identical to the Declaration of Principles of August 1993. It called for an almost complete Israeli withdrawal from the Gaza Strip and Jericho, to be followed shortly thereafter by the extension of Palestinian self-rule to the entire West Bank.

. . . . .

In that same month, December 1992, Rabin and Chief of Staff Lt.-General Ehud Barak decided on the expulsion of 415 Hamas and Islamic Jihad agitators. The expulsion, which was provoked by some particularly bold and successful strikes by these militant fundamentalist organizations against Israeli army and police, did not have the desired effect. The outpouring of sympathy for the deportees by the world media and the pressure on Israel to allow them to return (to which Rabin soon succumbed) encouraged not only the Muslims but also the PLO (including Fatah, Arafat's own faction) to continue their terrorist activities.

By the end of March, Rabin found himself in a critical position. Fifteen months had passed since his election to the premiership, and though he had pledged to achieve an autonomy agreement with the Palestinians within six to nine months, there had been no progress on that front. The talks with the Arab delegations in Washington—begun by his predecessor Yitzhak Shamir in the wake of the Madrid conference of October 1991—had been suspended; increased terrorist strikes had made "Black March" one of the worst months in Israel's history; the Hamas deportees were becoming folk heroes; and his popularity in the polls was at an all-time low.

It was at this juncture that Rabin was finally informed about the Oslo negotiations. Instead of calling them off, he instructed that they be continued. Technically, this instruction was a violation of the country's law, which prohibited official contacts with the PLO except with cabinet approval. No such approval was given. The government ministers were not even aware of the negotiations.

At the end of April, Rabin decided to test the authority and clout of the PLO's interlocutors in Oslo by demanding of them that no official PLO representatives participate in the multilateral talks on refugees scheduled to be held (purely coincidentally) in Oslo. When his demand was promptly met, he was impressed. Why this should have been his reaction is puzzling. Obviously, a direct appeal from the Israeli Prime Minister was a more important sign of recognition to the PLO than the presence of its official representatives at the multilateral negotiations. Nevertheless, Rabin felt that the move proved he was dealing with the PLO's top echelon.

The media greeted the PLO concession with surprise, especially when the Palestinian representatives came out of the multilateral meeting beaming, and Abu Ala, although not a participant, announced to the TV cameras that it had been a great success. The reason for this elation was not only the recognition afforded the PLO by Rabin, but the fact that for the first time a high-ranking Foreign Ministry official—Director General Uri Savir—had become involved in the secret talks.

These talks now proceeded with Rabin's full acquiescence. From now on, they would be headed by Savir, an expert on U.S.-Israel relations (he had served as Consul General in New York) who knew little about the PLO, and Yoel Singer, an Israeli member of a prominent Washington law firm who would later become the Foreign Ministry's legal adviser. The secrecy was complete. In addition to the negotiators themselves, only Avi Gil, Peres's administrative assistant, and Shlomo Gur, Beilin's assistant, were privy to all developments. To ensure confidentiality, they handled typing, airline tickets, and other administrative details without benefit of secretaries. That nothing leaked to the press was extraordinary, particularly in light of the repeated PLO announcements that meetings at a high level were taking place. The world, accustomed to PLO prevarications and exaggerations, accepted the Israeli denials.

As Beilin recalls it, at the time they all still believed that the purpose of the negotiations was to draft a proposal that would be signed by the official delegations to the peace talks in Washington, which on the Palestinian side, of course, did not formally include the PLO. The Israelis thought they were getting a behind-the-scenes PLO endorsement, nothing more. Indeed, on August 15, only five days before the Declaration of Principles was initialed in Oslo, Rabin said at a government meeting that he hoped "Israeli elements" (a euphemism for "peace-camp" ministers and other dovish politicians) would not undermine Washington's policy of dissociation from the PLO.

On August 20, at the Norwegian government's guest house, Holst and a few Norwegian colleagues hosted Peres, Gil, Savir, Singer, Hirschfeld, and Pundik, who were joined by Abu Ala and his assistants, for the signing ceremony. The Israelis were there for one of the most momentous diplomatic moves in the history of their country—without having consulted a single military authority, a single intelligence officer, or a single expert on Arab affairs. To be sure, Rabin himself had gone over every word (though only later would he realize, as he admitted publicly, that the document had left "hundreds" of issues untouched; later still, he would declare that "the legal formulations of Oslo are rubbish" and that "what will be decisive are the facts on the ground").

Toasts were offered by Savir, Abu Ala, and Holst. Peres, in Oslo on an official visit, had sneaked out of his hotel for the ceremony, but he was still reluctant to take an active part in signing an agreement with the PLO. Savir and Singer initialed for Israel, Abu Ala and an assistant for the PLO. Hirschfeld was asked to add his signature, as a tribute to his contribution. As fortune would have it, on that day nine Israeli soldiers were killed on the Lebanese border.

· · · · ·

Rabin's approval of an agreement with "PLO-Tunis," as he had always referred to the organization's government-in-exile, amazed many. But Rabin, while he originally doubted that such an agreement would ever be reached, had also always deemed contacts with the PLO useful. Even in the days when he served as Minister of Defense in the national-unity government under Prime Minister Yitzhak Shamir, he would advise Shamir: let the local Palestinian leadership run to Tunis (an illegal act) as much as they want. They think they are putting one over on us, but in truth we are using them to get PLO approval for the agreement we must reach with the inhabitants of the territories. Without such approval, nothing will move. This way we can secure PLO sponsorship without having to accept the PLO's official presence or its participation in implementing the agreement.

But the PLO knew better. This would soon become clear when Rabin now applied much the same principle to the Oslo talks, explicitly announcing that "the test of the agreement is in its being signed by the delegations to the peace talks in Washington"—that is, not by the PLO. In a speech to the members of his government coalition he explained the tactic in detail:

> For a long time I believed that the Palestinian inhabitants of the territories would achieve their own ability to negotiate. But after more than a year of negotiations I reached the conclusion that they could not.... That is why the talks in Oslo were with Palestinians who are not necessarily residents of the territories. But the signing of the agreement will be between the delegations [to the peace talks in Washington].

Beilin, too, affirmed the separation between the Palestinian delegation in Washington and the PLO. Asked how Israel could sign such a declaration before the PLO abolished the clauses in its charter calling for Israel's destruction, Beilin answered: "The delegation [in Washington] is not the PLO, so the question is irrelevant." (This was in stark contrast to the Labor party's old accusation that the Shamir government had opened the door to PLO participation by negotiating in Madrid with a delegation that was "PLO except for its name.")

The original intention, then, in Beilin's words, "was to put the agreement on the table in Washington without exposing the fact that it had been negotiated with the PLO in Oslo." But at this point the story broke, possibly leaked by the Norwegians, who were approaching a parliamentary election. (Holst's party won.) Then, to the Israelis' surprise, the head of the Palestinian delegation in Washington, Haidar Abdel Shafi, clearly acting in coordination with the PLO, refused to sign the document. Let those who cooked this up sign it, he said.

Queried on an Israeli television program about what would happen to the agreement if Shafi refused to sign it, Beilin replied, "Pay no attention to him. We'll find someone who will sign it." But since no one in the Palestinian delegation would dare sign the document without the PLO's permission, there was only PLO-Tunis to do so. This elementary point seems to have eluded Rabin.

He was, it also seems, unaware that, on the eve of the Madrid conference, Faisal Husseini (the unofficial head of the Palestinian delegation who—being a resident of Jerusalem—had been disqualified as an official negotiator by the Shamir government) informed the then-Secretary of State, James Baker, that if an agreement were reached, only the PLO would sign it, not the delegation. (Husseini himself apparently leaked this information to the Hebrew daily *Ma'ariv.*)

So now Rabin had in hand a document which would not be signed by the only people he wanted to sign it: the representatives (albeit unelected) of the 1.8 million Palestinians living in the territories. He had to decide whether to let this "historic moment" dissipate or to enter into an agreement with PLO-Tunis, an organization which considered itself, and was considered by most of the world, the government-in-exile of the state of Palestine.

. . . . .

Rabin, clearly feeling he had reached the point of no return, chose to sign. At this stage, to go back to his original policy would have meant that, having violated his vow not to deal with PLO-Tunis, he had emerged with nothing to show for it. This would have been a political disaster for him in Israel, and it was a price he was obviously not ready to pay.

To make final recognition of the PLO more palatable, however, he insisted on three minimal conditions, which even the most extreme Israeli doves had always said should precede negotiations with the PLO: Palestinian recognition of Israel's right to exist; the renunciation of terrorism by the PLO; and the cancellation of the clauses in the PLO charter calling for the destruction of Israel.

Only then did feverish negotiations begin, and during the next ten days they seemed to produce results. Israel and the PLO would officially recognize each other, Arafat would commit himself to changing the charter, and the PLO would both renounce and denounce terrorism. Ironically, had Shafi been willing to sign, nothing of this would have made its way into the agreement. Yet even so, the PLO, which had already achieved what it wanted most—namely, Israeli recognition—did not give Israel all it demanded.

Thus, Israel demanded that the PLO charter be declared "invalid." The PLO agreed only to a declaration that the offensive clauses "are now inoperative, and no longer valid." The difference was subtle, but enough to turn a determined repudiation into something that could be and, among Palestinians, would be read as a mere observation.

Israel also demanded cessation of "the armed struggle"—the standard PLO euphemism for terrorist activities, hallowed as a sacred means to a sacred end. The PLO adamantly and successfully refused. It also flatly rejected the Israeli demand to declare an end to the uprising, which the PLO calls "the blessed *intifada*." (A senior PLO source told the Hebrew daily *Ha'aretz* that the Israelis had not even asked for an end to the *intifada*, only to its more extreme manifestations.)

Peres insisted that the letters of mutual recognition to be exchanged by Arafat and Rabin include a pledge by Arafat to appeal to the Palestinian people to refrain from terrorism. But Peres was persuaded that it would be unseemly for Arafat to address his people through an agreement with Israel. Instead, the promise to make such an appeal was included in a letter to the Norwegian Foreign Minister, Jorgen Holst (who would die four months later).

Arafat's letter of recognition to Rabin also contained a pledge to punish members of the PLO who might disobey the order to suspend terrorist activity. This was demanded not by the Israelis, but by U.S. Secretary of State Warren Christopher, who felt he needed it to get the ban on the PLO repealed in Congress. (A curious last-minute attempt to acquire American sponsorship for the agreement was made by Peres during a quick trip to the U.S. But Christopher politely rejected the Israeli appeal. "The Norwegians are the sponsors," he asserted to the press.)

Once the PLO executive committee approved the Declaration of Principles, it was to be signed by Peres and the PLO's Abu Mazen at the State Department in Washington. But the PLO saw here an opportunity to get Arafat to the White House. The Clinton administration, hungry for a foreign-policy success, pounced on the idea with gusto. Rather than allow Peres to lead the Israeli delegation, it proposed to invite Rabin. At first Rabin said that he would not go. But when Christopher called him (at 6 A.M. on a Sabbath morning), he immediately changed his mind. This enabled Arafat—still officially a wanted terrorist in the U.S.—to appear in Washington as a head of government. Arafat must have been unprepared for the alacrity with which the U.S. accepted the idea. His plane, donated by Saddam Hussein and still boasting the Iraqi colors, had to be hurriedly repainted with Algerian colors, since Iraqi planes were banned in the U.S.

· · · · ·

At six o'clock in the morning of September 13, Ahmed Tibi—an Israeli Arab gynecologist who is Arafat's political adviser (a breathtaking case of dual loyalty)—was awakened by a call from his boss. "I haven't slept all night," said Arafat, according to Tibi. "If the PLO instead of the official Washington delegation is not named as the representative of the Palestinian side in the agreement, I won't sign it."

Hearing of Arafat's ultimatum, Peres at first threatened to leave Washington. But within minutes, says Tibi, "a compromise was found": Abu Mazen would write "PLO" on the document where the words

"Palestinian delegation" appeared. In Tibi's account, when Arafat heard that Peres had accepted this "compromise"—in fact, an Israeli capitulation—he was incredulous. "Are you sure they agree?" he asked Tibi. "The man, Peres, is standing next to me," responded Tibi. "So I send two kisses on your head," answered Arafat, and Tibi rushed to dress for the ceremony.

The Israelis were promised that Arafat would not wear a military uniform or carry a gun to the ceremony. When he boarded the plane in Tunis he was wearing a uniform, and carrying a gun. At the White House, he appeared without the gun, but the military uniform remained. The Israelis called it a green suit.

The upshot was that, desperate by now for anything that would seem like a success, Rabin had become an easy mark. Simply by causing the negotiations to bog down and denying Israel a partner who could sign an agreement, Arafat got Rabin to break cherished taboos and cross hallowed red lines. He also got Rabin to accept promises that would be forgotten almost as soon as they were made.

For example, disappointed by the PLO's refusal to declare an end to the "armed struggle" and the *intifada*, Israeli officials rationalized it as Arafat's need to "save face"; the commitments to Holst, they maintained, meant in effect a total end to violence. Yet in numerous PLO messages to the territories, culminating in a January call to Gaza activists, Arafat would vow that the *intifada* would "continue and continue and continue." And indeed, following the agreement there was to be no slackening either of *intifada* activities or of terrorism.

Again, in his letter to Holst, Arafat promised that he would make his appeal against violence as soon as the Declaration of Principles was officially signed. Not unreasonably, the Norwegians, Americans, and Israelis all expected him to do this in his speech at the signing ceremony on the White House lawn. Waiting for the magic words to be uttered any moment, Ehud Ya'ari, the Israel Television commentator who covered the proceedings, used every break in Arafat's speech to announce, "Now he will denounce terrorism ... now he will say it ... now he simply has to say it...." Only after the last paragraph did Ya'ari give up: "He is not saying it," he reported, crushed.

Nor would Arafat set a date for implementing the changes in the PLO charter to which he had committed himself. Nor did it seem likely that the necessary two-thirds majority could be found in the PLO "parliament," the Palestine National Council (PNC), to ratify such alterations. And in any case, Arafat himself would go on to declare that he had no intention of asking for a change in the charter. As his colleague Ziad Abu Zayyad would put it: "Asking us to abolish parts of the charter is like us asking you to abolish the Bible."

· · · · ·

Arafat was followed by the media throughout the day of the signing. What they did not report was that he made a broadcast to the Palestinian people through Jordanian television on that very day. In it, he mentioned neither a halt to terrorism nor peace or coexistence with Israel. Instead, he described the agreement as the first step "in the 1974 plan"— known by all Arabs as the "plan of phases" for the destruction of Israel.

He did not need to spell it out, for he could be confident that his audience would understand the implications: that the foothold the agreement had just given him would now open the way in short order to an independent Palestinian state in Gaza, Judea, and Samaria with Jerusalem as its capital; and that this would make it easier to continue the struggle for the "right of return" of between one and two million Palestinians to pre-1967 Israel, which they still regarded as their homeland.

Yet no Israeli government, not even the most leftist or the most dovish, would be able to accept such an outcome. Nor (despite the provision in the agreement of an interim period of autonomy) did the PLO have any intention of waiting for full sovereignty or settling for anything less. Therefore, the likelihood was that the deal would fall apart at an earlier stage, dashing the unrealistic expectations it had recklessly raised on both sides, bringing bitter and angry disappointment to Israelis and Palestinians alike, and leading not to peace but to a full-scale and very bloody showdown.

—March 1994

Douglas J. Feith

Land
for No Peace

T he 1993 Israel-PLO accord was supposed to bring on the new dawn of peace that optimists contended could be Israel's for the asking. Many Israelis, fatigued by decades of securing the land and themselves against Arab threats, military and terrorist, had come to regard the status quo as unbearable. Perhaps, they speculated, Palestinian-Arab leadership had evolved away from ideological anti-Zionism toward a pragmatic willingness to share the land with the Jewish state in peace. After the Soviet Union's collapse and the 1991 American-led attack on Iraq for its seizure of Kuwait, Israel's strategic strength and Yasir Arafat's political and economic weakness combined to make Israeli officials think they could test that hopeful proposition without undue risk.

The accord comprised, first, the Declaration of Principles (DOP), which was concluded on August 20, 1993 and signed by Arafat and Prime Minister Yitzhak Rabin at the White House on September 13, 1993; and, second, the mutual-recognition agreement embodied in the letters dated September 9, 1993 exchanged by Arafat, Rabin, and the Norwegian Foreign Minister. No one can doubt that these agreements are significant; but what exactly do they signify?

The DOP provides for the withdrawal of Israel's military forces from Gaza and Jericho and the transfer of governing authority for "education and culture, health, social welfare, direct taxation, and tourism" to an Arab Council "empowered to legislate." The DOP is often called the Gaza-Jericho accord, but this is misleading because the transfers of *governing* authority are not limited to Gaza and Jericho. On the contrary: the Council's jurisdiction will cover "the West Bank and the Gaza Strip as a single territorial unit, whose integrity will be preserved during the interim period"—i.e., "a transitional period not exceeding five years."

The Council, to be established following general elections, will assume the responsibilities Israel is relinquishing, but in the meantime authority rests with the PLO. "Palestinians of Jerusalem who live there will have the right to participate in the election process for the Council," and Jerusalem is one of the "issues that will be negotiated in the permanent-status negotiations."

Such Israeli concessions went far beyond the West Bank–Gaza Strip autonomy provisions of the 1978 Camp David accord signed by Israel's Menachem Begin and Egypt's Anwar Sadat. That accord designated the autonomy authority as an "administrative council" and withheld from it all legislative or proto-parliamentary powers. At Camp David, the Israeli government took care to specify that the aim was "to provide full autonomy *to the inhabitants*" (emphasis added) rather than to the territories as such, let alone to all "the West Bank and the Gaza Strip as a single territorial unit." Begin considered this distinction between autonomy for the inhabitants and autonomy for the territories important to prevent prejudicing the issue of Israel's right to assert claims regarding the territories in final-status negotiations. Israel did not, at Camp David, accept the PLO as an interlocutor. And it refused to make Jerusalem a topic for negotiation at any time.

Placing the 1978 accord side by side with the 1993 DOP highlights the historic and unprecedented nature of Israel's concessions in the latter agreement.

· · · · ·

What of the PLO'S concessions? The Arafat-Rabin agreements were not the first time the PLO chairman had acknowledged Israel's right to exist, declared the PLO'S acceptance of UN Security Council Resolutions 242 and 338, and promised to renounce anti-Israel terrorism. Arafat did all of that in December 1988 to win the PLO its official, open dialogue with the U.S. government. (Eighteen months later, Arafat's unwillingness to repudiate a PLO terrorist attack compelled the Bush administration to terminate the dialogue.)

Nor was this the first time the PLO had announced that it would consent to accepting authority in whatever portion of the territories became available to it. The Palestine National Council originally did that in the summer of 1974, when it formally resolved to combine diplomacy with armed struggle. In what came to be known as the "phased plan," the PLO leadership agreed that its principles were not offended by the dismantlement of Israel in stages and through diplomacy, rather than all at once and solely by military means.

Wherein, then, lay the much-heralded "breakthrough to peace" on Arafat's side? In the view of those who perceived one, the breakthrough was that this time Arafat actually meant what he said. (One Israeli official was quoted to the effect that quarrels within the PLO over Arafat's peace pledges were a sign that the pledges were not tactical but reflected a deep ideological change.) Skeptics were referred to the fact that Arafat's promises were now formulated explicitly (as if an explicit statement cannot be false). Also, those promises now included an unambiguous commitment to delete provisions in the Palestinian Covenant rejecting Israel's right to exist. Furthermore, Arafat had formally agreed, directly with the Israeli government, to an autonomy timetable that was supposed to defer for years into the future any demand for Arab sovereignty in the territories. And finally, not only would the PLO's own anti-Israel violence end, but Arafat would cooperate in keeping Hamas, Islamic Jihad, and other overt rejectionists in check.

None of these PLO promises was kept.

To begin with, the PLO did not amend its Covenant. Though accepted by Israel as leader of the organization deemed "representative of the Palestinian people," Arafat proved unable to command the requisite endorsement of his leadership from the Palestine National Council, the body empowered to amend the Covenant, or even from many of the top officials of his own Fatah faction of the PLO. After a number of his top PLO colleagues resigned or otherwise protested the Israel-PLO agreements, Arafat dropped whatever plans he had to propose amendment of the Covenant.

Secondly, in violation of its agreement to defer the demand for sovereignty, the PLO insisted upon immediate moves toward that goal. Thus, throughout the negotiations that produced the May 4 agreement on implementing the DOP, Arafat pressed for an expansive definition of "Jericho" (far broader than the bounds of the town itself), exclusive PLO control over border crossings, immediate removal of Jewish settlements, and implicit endorsement of PLO claims to Jerusalem.

Thirdly, in the months after the DOP was signed, there was intensified violence by Arabs against Jews, some of it perpetrated by Arafat's own Fatah faction. Nor did the PLO crack down on Hamas and other non-PLO extremists. In fact, open collusion among them was evident, including the publication of joint declarations, participation in demonstrations together, PLO demands for the release of arrested Hamas personnel, and announcement of new PLO-Hamas understandings on cooperation to remove Israel from the territories. Though Palestinian-Arab terrorism had plagued the land for nearly a century, every new attack now evoked defensive explanations that the actual target was the "peace process." (This led one Israeli wit to call for an end to the peace process so that he could get some peace.)

· · · · ·

Israeli government officials voiced frustration over this state of affairs, but they took pains not to sound accusatory. Shortly before the DOP was signed, Yossi Beilin, Israel's Deputy Foreign Minister, declared, "If there are problems on the way to implementing the agreement and if they cannot control their opposition and there is no order, we will say we can't go on." This reassuring theme was stressed repeatedly before the signing ceremony. On August 31, the *Washington Post* reported: "Peres told the Israeli parliament that Israel will not recognize the PLO unless it removes from its charter a call for armed struggle against Israel and halts violent attacks on Israeli targets." The next day, the *Wall Street Journal* reported:

> Mr. Beilin . . . also said that the DOP plan is conditional on the Palestinians being able to prevent Islamic fundamentalist groups who oppose the peace talks from carrying out terrorist attacks against Israel. . . .
>   Mr. Beilin . . . said that a key part of the "Gaza and Jericho first" plan is the fact that it is reversible.
>   Mr. Beilin continued, "As in any other agreement, there is the belief that both sides will be able to implement it and can be trusted, but if there is a clear violation, it will be more than understandable that we cannot adhere to it."

Nevertheless, when the PLO failed to control its opposition (and even its own elements), when there was terrorism and no order, and when the PLO otherwise violated the DOP and the mutual-recognition agreement, the Israeli government did not say, "We can't go on."

On September 13, the very day the DOP was signed in Washington, Jordanian television aired a speech by Arafat which, among other offensive features, explained his peace policy by reference to the phased plan:

O my beloved ones: do not forget that our Palestine National Council made the decision in 1974. It called for the establishment of national authority on any part of Palestinian soil that is liberated or from which the Israelis withdraw. It is the fruit of your struggle, sacrifices, and jihad. . . .

Brothers, beloved ones: Palestine is only a stone's throw away for a small Palestinian boy or girl. It is the Palestinian state that lives deep in our heart. Its flag will fly over the walls of Jerusalem, the churches of Jerusalem, and the mosques of Jerusalem.

They see the day indeed as a far-off event, but we see it quite near and we indeed are truthful.

This extraordinary statement was tantamount to Arafat's concluding his White House speech of conciliation with a loud and jeering "I take it back!" The Israeli government took it in stride, however, as it did the PLO's subsequent failure to amend the Covenant. Israel exerted itself to lure the PLO back to the table when the PLO walked away. Israel urged its U.S. supporters *not* to link PLO promises—for example, on the Covenant issue—to any waiver of various anti-PLO provisions of U.S. law. And Israel restrained itself and its U.S. supporters from pressing for a U.S. veto of the UN Security Council resolution condemning the massacre of Muslims by a Jew in Hebron, even though the resolution referred prejudicially to the territories as "Palestinian" land and designated Jerusalem as "occupied territory."

In light of the history of PLO terrorism and untruthfulness, and of Israeli defense-mindedness and distrust, it was stunning—one might even say disorienting—to see Israeli officials soliciting European and American financial support for the PLO, gesturing good will through the release of hundreds of suspected Palestinian-Arab terrorists, and muting their own and their public's outrage over continuing anti-Israel terrorism by the PLO. Students of military history are familiar with the fog-of-war phenomenon. Students of the Arab-Israeli conflict have, since September 13, 1993, come to know the fog of peace.

· · · · ·

What kind of strategy or rationale or theory underlies such a policy? The usual answer is "land for peace." But this longstanding concept has in important respects been transcended or shunted aside by the Israel-PLO accord and the implementation talks.

Israelis who view territorial withdrawal as the key to resolving the conflict between themselves and the Palestinian Arabs have generally done so on pragmatic grounds. The contention has been not so much that Israel lacks rights in the territories as that their retention, given the over-1.5-million Arab inhabitants, would swamp the Jewish state demographically. The classic formulation has been that holding on to the territories will ultimately destroy either the Jewish nature of the state, if the Arabs are given Israeli citizenship, or its democratic character, if they are not. Exponents of this view, most notably the present Foreign Minister, Shimon Peres, consistently maintained, however, that they would be willing to relinquish the militarily valuable territories to an Arab power only in return for peace and security.

But there was always a contradiction inherent in the demographic-bomb theory. If the Arab powers refused to grant Israel peace and security, would a proponent of that theory favor retaining the territory even though doing so would be suicidal, in that it would destroy either Israel's Jewish or its democratic nature? Clearly, underlying this position has always been a rationale not for trading territory for peace, but for unilateral withdrawal by Israel. The theory in effect tells Israel's enemies that they need not pay a price for the territories because Israel will either destroy itself by sitting tight, or up and leave for its own reasons, without demanding much (or perhaps anything) in return.

In the past, this contradiction was effectively finessed by the contention that the Palestinian Arabs (perhaps in confederation with Jordan) were in fact willing to offer Israel a secure peace if only the Israeli government, as a matter of policy, would agree to trade territory for it. Essential to a land-for-peace policy was a sequence of steps (and the order was important). First, Israel would renounce permanent control of the land, declaring its readiness to trade land for peace. Second, Israel's Arab interlocutors would make a credible and authoritative pledge of peace. And third, with this reliable peace promise in hand, Israel would effect the agreed-upon withdrawal.

This, in essence, was the policy the new Rabin government adopted when it came to office in 1992. In the so-called Madrid Process, the Rabin government, unlike its predecessor, made clear that it was willing to relinquish territory in return for peace. But after a year, the talks had produced no peace agreements. There was stalemate on all fronts. Mutual recriminations were rife. Anti-Israel violence was claiming numerous victims and provoking Israel into large-scale retaliations, such as the expulsion of 400 accused fundamentalist terrorists to Southern Lebanon in December 1992 and Operation Accountability in July 1993, which forced thousands of Arabs in Lebanon to evacuate their homes. Around the world, journalists and officials criticized these Israeli actions.

A land-for-peace policy had not produced the anticipated softening of Arab negotiating demands, and Israeli officials spoke with exasperation of their unhappiness that the Arabs refused to meet them halfway in the Washington talks.

If the Israeli government continued to insist on a credible and authoritative pledge of peace as a *precondition* of withdrawal, the prospect loomed that it would not be able, within its four-year term of office, to deliver to its citizens a new peace agreement or deliver them from the travails of the occupation. So the traditional idea of land for peace was set aside, and Israel concluded the deal embodied in the DOP.

It is noteworthy that the DOP was agreed upon and published by the Israeli government *before* the PLO and Israel had concluded the mutual-recognition agreement by which Arafat promised to respect Israel's right to exist; to renounce, prevent, and punish anti-Israel terrorism and violence; and to detoxify, as it were, the Palestinian Covenant. On September 1—that is, after the DOP was published but before the mutual-recognition agreement was achieved—Peres announced that Israel intended to implement the Declaration even if the PLO failed to make the peace pledges required for Israeli recognition: "The Declaration stands on its own legs. It doesn't need any further confirmation." The next day the *New York Times* reported: "Israeli officials say that if the two sides cannot agree on terms of mutual recognition in the near future, Israel would be ready to sign the accord anyway."

In other words, policy had evolved to the point where Israel was intent on beginning to withdraw from at least some of the territory *whether or not* it received a specific, authoritative promise of peace from the Arab side.

The deal, then, falls outside the traditional concept of land for peace. It treats Israeli withdrawals not as the reward, after the fact, for a clear-cut, credible, duly formalized, pacific change of heart on the part of an Arab interlocutor, as was the case in 1977 with Anwar Sadat, the President of Egypt. Rather, Israel is to withdraw in the hope that this will encourage such a change of heart and, if no such change occurs, then so be it.

· · · · ·

Though the case for unilateral withdrawal by Israel—now sometimes described euphemistically as a "divorce" from the territories—has greater internal consistency than the traditional land-for-peace idea, it puts Israel on a perilous course leading to grave disappointment and worse.

The traditional land-for-peace approach entailed danger for Israel because the land in question could serve as a staging area for terrorism, military attacks, or both, and because the promises given to Israel, even if sincere, would come from individuals who ruled undemocratically and could not commit their political successors. But the current approach of withdrawals-first-and-maybe-peace-later entails all these risks and more. For as the expression on Rabin's face made clear during the first famous handshake on the White House lawn, Israel can hardly take Arafat's credibility for granted. And even if it could, subsequent events have demonstrated that Arafat cannot win a reassuring margin of support for the deal from the PLO as a whole, or even from his own Fatah organization, let alone from the growing number of Palestinian Arabs who line up with Hamas, Islamic Jihad, and other non-PLO rejectionist groups.

Some Israelis dismiss these considerations. They believe that, even if the withdrawals do not resolve or even mitigate the Arab-Israeli conflict, Israel is better off confronting its future security problems without what they view as the encumbrance of the occupation. This is strongly implied when officials like Beilin refer to the territories as "a burden and a curse."

But unilateral withdrawal cannot produce the promised liberation from moral, military, or other problems. It will instead result in Israel's exchanging one set of problems for another. The material and moral burdens of the occupation—though not to be denied or belittled—are not a threat to Israel's existence. Neither, as 27 years of history attest, need they be fatal to Israel's democratic institutions or principles. They create strains, sometimes severe; but many democracies have suffered and survived strains from security threats, and Israel's commitment to a liberal rule of law remains robust.

On the other hand, territorial withdrawals that (1) reduce Israel's strategic depth; (2) deprive Israel of control over the Judean and Samarian highlands; (3) reduce Israel's time for mobilization in a crisis; (4) require greater reliance on preemption strategies; or (5) increase Israel's chances of being cut in half in a war will create problems of a far higher order. The often demoralizing psychological and economic burdens of the occupation will then be replaced by even more demoralizing psychological and economic burdens arising from physical insecurity and a hair-trigger national-defense posture.

It has been asserted that the Israel Defense Forces could easily handle any military threat Arafat and the PLO might pose from the territories. This is a reassurance that deserves to be credited—so long as current circumstances prevail. But if Islamic fundamentalist forces were to win additional political successes in countries like Egypt, Jordan, Syria, and Lebanon, and among the Palestinian Arabs themselves—hardly an inconceivable eventuality—the ability of Israel's enemies to exploit any territorial concessions made now to the PLO would increase substantially.

· · · · ·

There is yet another important issue in the negotiations: national rights. In debates over national-security policy, it is always useful to remind oneself of what one is aiming to secure. For a country like the United States or Israel, national security is far more than simply the physical survival of the citizenry. America is more than a land and a people: it is a society based on a constitution; it is an idea. Israel too is an idea. It is the fulfillment of the Zionist dream, the embodiment of the internationally recognized national rights of the Jewish people.

When contemplating a proposed concession by Israel, it is not enough to ask whether that concession would endanger the state's physical security. It is altogether proper for Israelis to ask themselves also whether the concession involves an undue relinquishment of national rights. This point was underlined for me by the comment of an Israeli friend—a strong proponent, by the way, of the Israel-PLO accord. He said:

> I have great sympathy for those Jews who value Hebron and Nablus, who have intense Zionist feelings about them. I personally don't share those feelings for those places, but I do share them for Jerusalem. If the Arabs were to say, "You Jews can have peace but you must give up Jerusalem," I would say that I'd rather have Jerusalem. If it ever got to the point where I would rather have peace than Jerusalem, I would move to the United States.

A statement like this reminds us that there is more at stake in the negotiations than peace and the physical security of Israelis. One cannot define the national security of Israel without reference to the principles of Zionism, any more than one could define the national security of the United States without reference to the principles of the U.S. Constitution. Though it is common for nations to trade assets with one another for purposes of commerce or to solve quarrels, there are some things that a nation can never trade away unless it is willing to change its basic character. Nations that try to buy peace with aggressive neighbors by trading national rights often wind up with neither sovereignty nor peace.

· · · · ·

Much has been made of the fact that the Arab parties are for the first time willing to negotiate peace with Israel openly. That is something; but does it establish that the Arab intent is peaceable? After all, every ambitious and aggressive dictator for the last 100 years engaged in highly publicized peace talks: Lenin, Stalin, Hitler, Saddam Hussein, and Slobodan Milosevic all participated in peace negotiations and used them to pursue belligerent designs.

Nor is there any guarantee that the follow-up negotiations will succeed in carrying the DOP into full effect. Notwithstanding the lengthy, complex, and bitterly negotiated May 4 implementation agreement, the overarching Israel-PLO accord of September 1993 could disintegrate, as have other diplomatic gossamers of the Middle East from the 1919 Feisal-Weizmann agreement to the 1983 Israel-Lebanon treaty.

Israeli withdrawal from the territories is beginning. Whether it can continue and to what extent are questions that hinge largely on Arafat's credibility and authority. Though the avant-garde of Israel's unilateral-withdrawal school may say to itself, "We will not let Arafat block our withdrawal, no matter what," the general Israeli public has been taught to expect reliable peace and security commitments in any trade for territory. It is crucial, then, that the PLO provide political cover: enough concessions from Arafat to give the appearance of mutuality; at a minimum, sufficient controls on political violence to allow Israeli forces to go on withdrawing from the territories without precipitating outbreaks of mayhem and killings; a decent interval.

Yet the more influential the unilateral-withdrawal school has appeared to be in Israel, the less Arafat has been inclined to make any concessions at all. Indeed, for more than half a year after he signed the DOP, Arafat devoted himself to taking back important concessions—for example, by raising issues like the settlements and Jerusalem. Given Arafat's record, traits, and various incapacities (including his lack of authority over even his core constituency), there remains a substantial possibility that the negotiating dynamics will ultimately produce not a final settlement under the Israel-PLO deal, but an unraveling.

If this unraveling should occur, Israeli advocates of unilateral withdrawal will lose the valuable cover provided by the peace process, but they may—in the open, as it were—succeed in winning their essential point. Perhaps Israel will make further withdrawals and additional concessions even without credible and authoritative moves toward peace by Arafat and the PLO. If it does, its Arab enemies may take this as confirmation that unremitting hostility and violence, having driven the Jews from the territories, can also drive them the rest of the way out of Palestine. In much of the Arab world, the Crusader analogy—two centuries were required to wear down and expel the Crusaders from the Holy Land, this analogy goes, and Arabs should be prepared to do the same with the Jews no matter how long it takes—is frequently invoked and is vivid and inspirational.

Israel may thus discover that the problem is not the intransigence or the flexibility of its own policies or the shape of its boundaries. Rather, the problem is whether its neighbors have the political leadership and the good will to sustain peace with a Jewish state on what, according to their religious and cultural convictions, is *their* land, *Arab* land—that is, anywhere in Palestine. If, contrary to all benevolent hopes, it transpires that those neighbors are not so willing, Israelis will have to tap into their Zionist heritage to find enough conviction and fortitude to defend themselves, for however long may be necessary, against hostility and violence, against *intifadas* and wars, if they are to preserve their state.

—*June 1994*

Dore Gold

Where Is the
Peace Process Going?

Still another moment of transition is occurring in Israel as the government of Yitzhak Rabin moves toward implementing the next phase of the agreement it struck in September 1993 with the PLO in Oslo. As at earlier stages, the arrival of this moment has been beset by delays—for reasons that are not far to seek. Although incidents of Arab terror abated sharply in the months just prior to the deadline for this further extension of Palestinian self-rule, the previous year had been marked by a tremendous increase in anti-Israel violence, and within Israel itself the feeling had become widespread that the entire Oslo "process" had failed—indeed, had perhaps been misconceived from the outset.

That judgment was not limited to Rabin's parliamentary opposition and its supporters in the electorate. The Israeli military, normally extremely reticent about political matters, was quite blunt about the unfolding implementation of the Oslo accords in Gaza and Jericho. Thus, on May 3 of this year, Amnon Shahak, chief of staff of the Israel Defense Force (IDF), told the newspaper *Yediot Ahronot:* "The security situation in Gaza is far from being something to which one can give a passing grade." Shaul Mofaz, who as head of the IDF's southern command has operational responsibility for the Gaza area, told the same newspaper two weeks earlier that Arafat "has not met the conditions of the agreement he signed." In Mofaz's words, "Arafat ... has failed, failed, failed."

The Israeli man in the street was no less outspoken. If ordinary Israelis had one main priority which they hoped their government would address in any peace settlement, it was personal security; in 1992, the Likud government of Yitzhak Shamir had fallen from power after a spate of knifing incidents that sapped public confidence. But whereas, during the worst years of the *intifada*, Israeli fatalities in terrorist incidents had ranged from 14 to 40 annually, in the past year Israeli fatalities shot up to over 80. Moreover, the sporadic knifings of the pre-1992 period were now replaced with a far more lethal form of terrorism: bus bombings. And these attacks were directed for the most part not at Israeli settlements in the administered territories but at the populace in the heart of pre-1967 Israel. (Some of the more spectacular terrorist incidents, like the kidnapping and murder of Nahshon Waxman, were in fact the work of Palestinians released from Israeli prisons after Oslo.) As two leading Israeli journalists concluded in mid-May: "From the start, Rabin marketed the Oslo agreement as an answer to a security problem. In this sense, the agreement has been revealed to be until today a failure."

. . . . .

If such sentiments are justified, it bodes ill for the next stage of the Oslo agreement, no matter how warily Israel enters into it and despite temporary respites from terrorism. Are they justified?

To answer that question properly, one has to go back to the beginning of the process by which Israel got itself entangled in its almost-two-year-old agreements with the PLO. Until now this has not been easy to do, for the literature on the genesis of the process is, surprisingly, rather scant. Each of the other major turning points in the country's recent history—the 1978 Camp David accords between Israel and Egypt, the 1982 Lebanon war, the *intifada* that erupted in 1987—quickly generated a half-dozen or more books analyzing the political forces involved and the implications of the events in question. By contrast, the 1993 Declaration of Principles (DOP) between Israel and the PLO, probably the most important diplomatic agreement negotiated in Israel's short history and a story that begs for interpretation and insight, went relatively untreated except for a few memoirs by those involved.

Now, however, David Makovsky, the diplomatic correspondent of the *Jerusalem Post*, has come the closest to doing for Oslo what Bob Woodward and Carl Bernstein did in the United States for Watergate. Unlike the mass-market books that come out of the Washington press corps, though, Makovsky's *Making Peace With the PLO* is a work of scholarship. Makovsky is especially careful not to allow himself to get drawn into the pre-Oslo debate within Israel over whether peace with the Palestinians was possible, and he is equally careful to avoid the even more polarized debate that has taken place in Oslo's aftermath. He does not try to judge the Israeli government's decision-making process, only to understand and explain it.

Nevertheless, and despite its restraint, *Making Peace With the PLO* is fascinating to read, and it offers a vital resource to anyone wishing to reach his own conclusions about what exactly happened back in September 1993, and what it means.

The outline of the story Makovsky tells is well-enough known. A secret dialogue takes place in early 1993 between two obscure Israeli academics and the PLO in Oslo, Norway. The academics are connected with Israel's Deputy Foreign Minister, Yossi Beilin, a man whom Prime Minister Rabin had dismissed years earlier on Israeli television as the "poodle" of his arch-rival, Shimon Peres. Now, with Peres serving, ironically enough, as Rabin's Foreign Minister, the dialogue evolves into a full-blown negotiation that, with Rabin's apparent blessing and support, circumvents the official peace talks between Israel and the Palestinians going on simultaneously in Washington. With astonishing rapidity an agreement is concluded by mid-summer, and the DOP is rushed to Washington for signing. The full prestige of the Clinton presidency is mobilized to back the accord, culminating in the Rabin-Arafat handshake on the White House lawn.

Those are the bare bones; *Making Peace With the PLO* does much to flesh them out.

One thing that emerges with particular clarity from Makovsky's account is that the initial contacts between Israel and the PLO were put, fatefully, into the hands of people with a far greater interest in economics than in security, and with no experience or training as negotiators. That was certainly the case with the two academics, Yair Hirschfeld of Haifa University and Ron Pundik of the Hebrew University, who pioneered the Oslo channel. In a clear reflection of their interests and biases, the text of the DOP was full of references to economic-cooperation projects and joint-business ventures. And the Norwegian sponsors of the contacts were equally prone, as Makovsky notes, to invoke "the experience of the European Community in transforming political relations by institutionalizing shared economic endeavor."

Yet, on the assumption that the Rabin government was irretrievably bent on opening a channel to the PLO, there were other possible routes to go. Shlomo Gazit, the former chief of military intelligence who had been IDF coordinator for the territories back in 1967, had PLO contacts, as did Ephraim Sneh, a Labor-party member of the Knesset (MK) who once headed Israel's civil administration in Judea and Samaria. Either of these men would have brought to the discussions more military experience than what was on offer from Hirschfeld and Pundik. Or Rabin could have picked a loyal political appointee with a background in security and sent him to Norway along with the two academics.

As things stood, however, every major Israeli security organization—the Mossad, the General Security Services, Israeli military intelligence, as well as the IDF—was cut out of the loop; as Makovsky stresses, Oslo lay exclusively in the hands of the two academics from January until mid-May. On May 21, a week after Rabin had given his consent to the proceedings, the first Israeli official, Uri Savir, director general of the Foreign Ministry, joined the talks; yet Savir, although he could make a political assessment for his boss, Shimon Peres, had not participated in previous Arab-Israeli negotiations. Only on June 11 were the talks further strengthened on the Israeli side by the inclusion of Joel Singer, who had served in the advocate-general's office of the IDF and had provided staff work for military talks with Egypt in the late 1970's. But this left very little time for official input; the DOP was completed and initialed by both parties in Oslo on August 20.

In other words, the truly serious phase of Oslo was not more than six weeks in duration. In an interview with Makovsky, Joel Singer (who is now the legal adviser to the Foreign Ministry) conceded that what had gone before had made his job that much more difficult: "If someone who is not a doctor is performing an appendectomy and in the middle of the operation he turns it over to you, you cannot just start from scratch."

But the real problem with the two academics was not their lack of negotiating skills; after all, as Makovsky observes, they had "received only minimal instructions from Beilin" and certainly had not been given any mandate to reach an agreement. Their chief role, at least at first, was to test the PLO's seriousness and to ascertain its true position. But *just here* lay the weakness of the whole enterprise. Makovsky writes:

> Rabin was highly dependent for information regarding the Oslo negotiations upon the two men who were most intimately involved in the evolution of the Oslo process and therefore had the greatest stake in its success: Peres and Beilin.

And Peres and Beilin were dependent, in turn, on the two academics. All four of Rabin's "evaluators," in other words, were true believers in both the possibility and the desirability of a "dialogue" with the

PLO. For any one of them to have concluded, after initial discussion, that the contact with Arafat should be discontinued would have meant burying one of the central items of faith on the Israeli Left. In other words, Rabin, to say the least, did not have the benefit of impartial advisers.

· · · · ·

What might such advisers have told him? One of the underlying assumptions of Oslo was that the PLO would have both the will and the capacity to fight the extremists in Hamas and Islamic Jihad, and hence protect Israel from terror. Makovsky quotes Joel Singer: "They [the PLO] kept saying all the time that Arafat could and would stop terrorism ... that Arafat would make the difference." After Oslo was signed, Rabin assured the Israeli public that the PLO would know how to take care of the fundamentalists, and, as he put it in his famously blunt manner, Arafat would not be hampered by the Israeli human-rights lobby and the Supreme Court. Yet independent analysis might have warned Rabin that this would not be the case. As Makovsky writes in one of his strongest judgments concerning the first months of the agreement's implementation, "This appears to be one of the big miscalculations of Oslo."

It is easy to reconstruct how the miscalculation transpired. Across the Middle East, from Algeria to Egypt, Arab nationalist regimes were facing a militant Islamic challenge. Most had not hesitated to unleash the full fire-power of their internal-security forces against armed fundamentalist factions. In the 1980's, moreover, Israel itself had created a South Lebanese Army to fight Hezbollah. Why could not something like this be recreated in the Gaza Strip, and later extended to the West Bank? Since the DOP was to be implemented in stages, Arafat would have built-in incentives for cooperating with Israel against Hamas—good behavior would mean getting the next chunk of territory under his control that much sooner.

But things did not work out as the architects of Oslo expected. Elsewhere in the Arab world, extreme Islamist forces had been challenging political establishments in place since the 1950's. Arafat, by contrast, was only getting started, and was immeasurably weaker than any Arab head of state.

Nor, more significantly, was Arafat's own calculus what the Rabin government imagined it would be. After the signing of the DOP, terrorist attacks were regularly followed by summit meetings at which Rabin would grimace, invoke the displeasure of Washington, and demand better performance by the Palestinian police. For Arafat, though, as unpleasant as these meetings could be, they were clearly preferable to the full-scale Palestinian civil war that a crackdown on the fundamentalists might have sparked.

Nor was even that all. It soon became evident that Rabin did not possess any real power of sanction against Arafat. To suspend the agreement itself—that is, to admit to failure—would be to incur an enormous political price at home that Rabin was clearly not prepared to pay. And even if the agreement *were* suspended, Arafat would not have lost much; the DOP, which he had negotiated in weakness, had gotten him Gaza and Jericho, and if the negotiations over the rest of the interim-status arrangements should be canceled, the possibility still lay open for jumping directly to final-status talks.

That, at least, is how things unfolded. What Makovsky's description makes clear is that any number of people might have told Rabin there was a good chance they would unfold in just that way.

. . . . .

Other eventualities might have been anticipated as well. Makovsky does not get heavily involved in the economic assumptions behind Oslo—the area where the experts were supposed to enjoy a professional advantage—yet here, too, grave errors were made.

In particular, there was an expectation of a major cash windfall: international aid would rain on the occupied territories, and a new Singapore would arise from the sands of Gaza. As noted above, this scenario had political implications: with Gaza industrialized, thousands of new jobs created, and the standard of living on the rise, fewer young people would be attracted to the ranks of Hamas and Islamic Jihad. Or so at least the logic ran. Economic growth was seen as a good in itself, and also as a precursor of political and military security.

In reality, during the first six months of the Palestinian administration, the standard of living in the Gaza Strip did not rise—it fell by some 25 percent. Continued terrorist action forced Rabin repeatedly to close off Israel to Palestinian workers, and within Gaza itself nowhere near enough new jobs were created. Although some recent local investment by the upper strata of Gazan society has generated more construction activity, it has been of insufficient scale to affect any large number of the Gazan refugees. In the end, terror and security considerations have dictated economic conditions, not the reverse.

. . . . .

Finally, Oslo would prove from the very beginning to have highly dele-terious effects on the status of Jerusalem.

Ever since 1967, Israeli governments had been prepared to discuss the rights of various religions to the holy places of Jerusalem. But no Israeli government prior to that of Yitzhak Rabin ever expressed an explicit and unqualified readiness to put Jerusalem itself on the table. This is what the DOP did in making the city a subject for negotiations with the opening of final-status talks scheduled (according to the origi-nal timetable) for May 1996.

Rabin's defenders might say there was a precedent for this: Yitzhak Shamir had gone to the Madrid peace conference in 1991 with the under-standing that all sides could bring any subject at all to the table. But how-ever reckless this might have seemed at the time, Shamir had no inten-tion of giving up control of the negotiating agenda, which in diplomacy is the first line of defense in protecting assets a nation does not want to concede. It was this outer line that fell at Oslo. Whether the Israelis real-ized it or not, the Palestinians certainly did, and celebrated the fact. In the words of PLO negotiator Nabil Shaath:

> [T]he Israelis up to this agreement never accepted that the final sta-tus of Jerusalem be on the agenda of the permanent status negoti-ations.... This [the DOP] calls into question the legality and final-ity of their annexation.
>
> Faisal al-Husseini was even more explicit: In the Oslo accords it was established that the status of Jerusalem is open to negotiations on the final arrangement, and the moment that you say yes to nego-tiations, you are ready for a compromise.

Of course, no more than Yitzhak Shamir did Yitzhak Rabin have any intention of giving up an inch of Jerusalem to the PLO. To the con-trary, he looked to the DOP as an instrument that would help protect Israel's position in the city—specifically, by allowing Jericho to evolve into an alternative administrative center for the Palestinians. But the PLO quickly installed two ministers of the Palestinian Authority (PA) inside Jerusalem itself. One of them, Faisal al-Husseini, now minister without portfolio, converted his family's property, known as Orient House, from an Arab-studies society to an administrative center at which major for-eign dignitaries were received. The PA also opened at least five other institutions in Jerusalem. The PA's security chief in Jericho, Jibril Rajoub, regularly sent his men into East Jerusalem to seize Palestinians and bring them to his headquarters for interrogation; by the end of June 1994, as

Rabin himself admitted in response to a parliamentary inquiry, some 200 Palestinian security personnel were operating in East Jerusalem. All these acts violated explicit clauses in the Oslo and Gaza-Jericho agreements, but Rabin did not combat them.

To judge by Makovsky's account, Arafat deserves high marks for successfully manipulating the Israeli Prime Minister over the Jerusalem issue. Essentially he pursued a double track, ordering the Palestinian delegation at the official peace talks in Washington to demand that the PLO be given some jurisdiction in Jerusalem already in the interim phase, while instructing his people in Oslo to take a more moderate position and agree to put off discussion of arrangements in the city until the beginning of final-status talks. Faced with a hard line in Washington, and seemingly greater flexibility in Oslo, Rabin gravitated toward the latter.

Arafat's Jerusalem ploy appears to have been behind Rabin's decision in May 1993 to upgrade the Oslo talks to the official governmental level. Indeed, one might say that an Israeli willingness to put Jerusalem on the table and at least theoretically envisage its future division is what finally made Oslo possible—surely not what Rabin had in mind, but just as surely something that cooler heads might have pointed out to him at the time, had they been consulted.

· · · · ·

In light of what Makovsky tells us, it is hardly any wonder that so many in Israel came to the conclusion by May of this year that Oslo represented a dead end. For the implementation of the DOP manifestly *had* failed to enhance Israeli security; failed to improve Palestinian well-being and hence reduce grievances; and failed to protect Jerusalem from the penetration of the PLO. Nevertheless, despite this general failure, the Rabin government persisted in its course, and made clear its intention of moving forward to the DOP's next stages. Why? The answer comes in several parts.

While the conservative portion of the Israeli political community has all along viewed Oslo as a fundamental if not a catastrophic blunder, some on the Left have stressed that, no matter how flawed it may be at any point in its implementation, it represents the correct strategic path. This has been implicit in Rabin's own rhetoric. After virtually each terrorist attack last year, he voiced his conviction that the only way to solve the Israeli-Palestinian conflict was through a "separation" of the two peoples. To that end, Oslo has been the means.

Many Israelis, indeed, Left, Right, and Center alike, are attracted by the notion that the Palestinians can be put behind some enormous fortification near the pre–June 1967 borders—a kind of Great Wall of China on the Green Line. For those on the Left who adhere to this view, the real barrier to success has been not the inability or the refusal of the PLO to adhere to the provisions of the DOP, but rather the existence in the territories of Israeli settlements built during the years of Likud rule—settlements which Rabin was, at least at first, reluctant to give up. As Makovsky writes, "In private discussions, Israeli negotiators in Oslo admitted that negotiating a quick divorce would have been their preference, but the refusal of Rabin to dismantle settlements at an early stage stood as an impediment." From this it would seem to follow that the way to deal with Oslo's failures is not to discard the agreement but, on the contrary, to *accelerate* the process of "separation."

In fact, however, all this talk of separation is just another way to avoid confronting Oslo's central problem. Separation is based on the principle that good fences make good neighbors. But Israel's history—indeed, the history of every nation in the world—shows that what is true is precisely the reverse: good neighbors make good fences. Where, as with Jordan, Israel enjoys such relatively good neighbors, fences supply security. Where it has bad neighbors, as in Lebanon, fences are wholly inadequate, and successive Israeli governments have had to introduce "security zones" to protect the country's border.

The architects of Oslo thought they could simply ignore the fact that every single one of the cruxes of the Israeli-Palestinian conflict—Jerusalem, borders, the fate of Palestinian refugees—remained unresolved. Instead, they proceeded to treat Arafat as though he were already the head of a neighboring state with which Israel happened to have a few, wholly containable, differences. As a thought experiment, this may have had something to recommend it; in reality, it foundered drastically on its own radically mistaken premise.

· · · · ·

Where, then, is the peace process going? Few would advocate that a future Israeli government should return to the Gaza Strip. But the current focus is on the West Bank, which, unlike Gaza, is right next to Israel's major population centers, as well as to 80 percent of the country's industrial capacity; whatever happens there bears on Israel's security, and indeed on its day-to-day existence, in the most direct way imaginable, and the perils are obviously enormous.

For one thing, as Yaakov Amidror, head of analysis for military intelligence, has acutely pointed out, the withdrawal of the IDF from West Bank cities, called for in the next phase of the agreement, may well *reduce* the PA's incentive to quell anti-Israel violence; terrorist organizations will no longer have to worry about local countermeasures by the Israeli military. But that is by no means all.

When the DOP was reached, it appeared that Israel had definitively abandoned its historic (under-the-table) alliance with Jordan, and from now on would give pride of place to its new relationship with the PLO. King Hussein himself stepped in to correct this distortion by completing his own agreement with Israel during 1994. Now, however, Israel appears about to place in power in the West Bank a political movement—the PLO—openly hostile to the Hashemite throne in Amman, thereby undermining both Israel's own interest and that of the United States in maintaining a moderate buffer state between the radicalism of the Fertile Crescent and Saudi Arabia's northwestern frontier.

One might have imagined an alternative course of action, and correspondingly different outcomes. Even today, when it is very difficult to envision a full-scale Jordanian role in the West Bank, one can still speculate whether many West Bank Palestinians might not prefer a tie with a strong, stable Jordan to one with Arafat's weak and chaotic Gaza. They might, indeed, have preferred such an arrangement even before the DOP, though it would have been impossible for them to say so. In light of what has occurred since Oslo, and what unfortunately appears likely to unfold in the next stage of implementation, is it inconceivable that West Bank Palestinians might yet begin to see their self-interest in more pragmatic and less ideologically charged terms?

For that to happen, however, and for all the interested parties in the region to be in a position to seek better alternatives than today's, the DOP would have to be permitted to lapse. But the chances of *that* happening, so long as the architects of Oslo are directing Israel's peace policy, remain slim indeed.

In the short run, therefore, one must look to other avenues. One thing that would have at least a somewhat salutary effect on the flawed Oslo agreements is a reordering of their priorities, giving primacy to the security needs of Israel in the next, crucial phase of implementation. Here, as David Makovsky's doleful chronicle reminds us, lies the heart of the Oslo "miscalculation." But it very much remains to be seen whether such a reordering will be put into place in the months ahead.

—*August 1995*

Hillel Halkin

The Rabin Assassination: A Reckoning

As a voter for the Labor party and Yitzhak Rabin in the 1992 elections and a politically angry man for the past two years, I found myself growing angrier and angrier the week after his assassination on November 4, 1995. The angrier I grew, the more I argued with everyone around me, and the more I argued, the angrier it made me. Not, like everyone else, at the assassin and those said to have incited him, but at the Labor party, and at the Israeli Left, and even at the murdered man himself, who was certainly not responsible for the thick sludge of sentimentality, so far from his own personal style (though not from that of his speechwriters), in which he was being quickly shrouded. I must have seemed a very unpleasant person. I may seem one to you now.

A large part of the sentimentalization in the days after the Rabin assassination lay in the event's being treated as, above all, a violation of the Sixth Commandment. "How could such a murderer have come from our midst?" and "What Jew would kill a Jew over land?" were the two questions most often asked in Israel, while, when Ted Koppel brought his *Nightline* to Jerusalem the week after the assassination, he billed the special broadcast as "Thou Shalt Not Kill."

This is sentimental because, though murder is a frightful crime, large numbers of men and women whose right to live is as great as that of the Prime Minister of Israel are the barely noticed victims of murder every day. In Israel alone, the police blotters show that dozens of Jews are killed annually by Jews without *Nightline*'s paying attention. And what, if not land, has been the single greatest motive for killing in human

45

history? What, if not the struggle for land, has caused tens of thousands of Jews and Arabs to be killed in the Middle East?

Was it not a struggle for land that made Yitzhak Rabin join the Palmah, the elite fighting force of Jewish Palestine, as a young man, and thus begin the military career that led to his becoming Prime Minister of Israel? Was it not for the control of land that, as Prime Minister, he continued a military presence in Lebanon which in 1995 alone resulted in the deaths of over twenty Israeli soldiers? If land is never a legitimate reason for killing, every soldier who fights for the defense of his country is a murderer.

What made Yitzhak Rabin's assassination exceptionally atrocious was not its being a murder but its being a cataclysmic political blunder.

It was so, firstly, because—as Likud leader Benjamin Netanyahu put it—democratically chosen governments are changed by elections, not by assassinations. Break that rule once and democracy is imperiled—and an undemocratic Israel cannot prosper, no matter how much or how little land it commands.

And it was so, secondly, because what it most damaged was the public standing of the critics of the Oslo peace process, to whose extreme wing the assassin Yigal Amir belonged. Had Amir wished to deliver a crushing blow to these critics, he could not have found a better way. That is why a friend of mine in America, a far more unequivocal opponent of the peace process than I, faxed me the week of the killing: "I would gladly see the bastard hang who prevented the people of Israel from voting against Rabin."

· · · · ·

Equally sentimental was the instant mythologization of Yitzhak Rabin as a knight of peace in shining armor.

The day after the assassination I talked with a different friend, an Israeli Arab. "I'm sorry it happened," he said, "but you can't expect me to feel sad for Rabin."

"Why not?" I asked.

"Because," he said, "in the late 1980s I happened to be in Tulkarm [a city on the West Bank] one day at the beginning of the *intifada,* when Rabin, who was then Minister of Defense, gave his famous order to the army to 'break the arms and legs' of Palestinians. And what I saw in Tulkarm were broken arms and legs. Children's too. That order was not meant metaphorically."

Indeed it was not, as many Israelis who carried it out can testify.

It has been said that Yitzhak Rabin had a change of heart and came out of the *intifada* a different man, convinced of the need for a reconciliation with the Palestinians. That may be. But in the summer of 1993, after his conversion supposedly took place and Israeli and PLO negotiators were meeting secretly in Oslo, Rabin, now Prime Minister, launched Operation Accountability, a massive retaliatory artillery bombardment that caused great civilian destruction in dozens of Lebanese villages accused of harboring Hezbollah guerrillas. He was then what he had always been and remained until his death, several days before which he almost certainly ordered the murder of Islamic Jihad leader Fat'hi Shiqaqi in Malta—namely, a highly pragmatic soldier and politician who had no special liking for violence but no compunctions about using it when it served tactical or strategic ends.

· · · · ·

I voted for Yitzhak Rabin in 1992 because, like many Israelis, I felt that the situation in the West Bank and Gaza had reached an intolerable point and that the Likud government was incapable of changing it. In terms of change, I was prepared to go farther than most Rabin voters. In an article published in *Commentary* over twenty years ago ("Driving Toward Jerusalem," January 1975), I had advocated, subject to certain conditions, the establishment of a Palestinian state along Israel's 1967 borders, and in 1992 I still held to this opinion. I still hold to it today.

Why, then, did I react with such anger to the Israeli-PLO agreement when it was announced in September 1993? Because it was obvious to me immediately that the Labor party had lied to the Israeli public; that it was either continuing to lie to it, or lying to itself, or both; and that all these lies were highly dangerous.

In its official 1992 campaign platform, Labor had declared:

> Israel will continue and complete negotiations with authorized and agreed-on Palestinians *from the territories occupied by Israel since 1967* [emphasis added].... There is a need for an agreement in a Jordanian-Palestinian framework ... and not a separate Palestinian state west of the Jordan.... Jerusalem will remain united and undivided under Israeli sovereignty.... The Jordan Valley and the western shore of the Dead Sea will be under Israeli sovereignty.... In any peace agreement with Syria, Israel's presence and control, both military and in terms of settlements, will continue [on the Golan Heights].

Let us set aside the question of the Golan Heights, even though Yitzhak Rabin's violation of his campaign promises in the course of his negotiations with President Hafez Assad was only partially compensated for by his announced commitment to holding a national referendum before signing a peace treaty with Syria. Let us speak instead of Oslo and the Palestinians.

The Labor party lied to the Israeli public because its 1992 platform clearly ruled out negotiations, let alone a comprehensive political settlement, between Israel and the PLO, which in 1992 was based not in the territories but in Tunis and which had been considered by all previous Israeli governments a terrorist organization not to be treated with. And since the PLO had stated repeatedly before Oslo, and continued to state after it, that its immediate goal was the creation of an independent Palestinian state in Gaza and the entire West Bank with East Jerusalem as its capital, there were only two explanations of Israeli thinking at Oslo. One was that Yitzhak Rabin and his government had secretly decided to acquiesce in the establishment of such a state, thereby reneging on the rest of their campaign pledges regarding the future of the occupied territories. The other was that they believed the peace process could be brought to a successful conclusion without yielding to the PLO's main territorial and political demands.

Let us first consider the second of these possibilities. In its final-stage negotiations with the Palestinians, supposedly set to begin later this year, can Israel simply declare: "Gentlemen, you are not getting a state and you are not getting Jerusalem and other areas, and you can either take or leave what we are giving you"?

In theory, of course, it can. In practice, the Palestinians, under the terms of the Oslo agreement, will by then have nearly 30,000 armed policemen in the West Bank and Gaza, close to the number of combat soldiers in Israel's standing army. Will Israel be prepared to risk engaging this force in armed conflict if a political impasse is reached?

This question, when put to supporters of the peace process, is met by a snort. It is absurd to think, one is told, that 30,000 policemen with rifles could offer serious resistance to a well-trained army with tanks and aircraft.

It is the snorters, however, who are being disingenuous if they imagine three divisions of Palestinian policemen will march on Jerusalem while the Israeli air force pounds them from above. These policemen can be divided into thousands of small cells of guerrilla fighters comprising five or ten members each. At the peak of the *intifada* there were probably never more than ten or twenty armed units of this size operating at any given moment in the occupied territories. Dozens of Israelis were killed by them. It took months to hunt down some of these bands; tanks and aircraft had little to do with the matter.

Would Yitzhak Rabin—who, we are told, was psychologically shaken to the core by the *intifada*—have been ready to expose Israel to a prolonged period of armed violence, possibly hundreds of times greater than that of the *intifada*, in order to keep his campaign promises regarding Jerusalem and the Jordan Valley, when he had already violated other key pledges in the same paragraph? Will his successor, Shimon Peres, be ready to do so if it should prove necessary?

· · · · ·

But, we are told, it will not prove necessary—because already at Oslo the Rabin government knew it was agreeing to the establishment of a Palestinian state in Gaza and the entire West Bank ruled from Jerusalem, and all its protestations to the contrary, at the time and subsequently, were not to be taken seriously.

"Honestly," said an Israeli to me during the week after the assassination, "you are being hopelessly naive. You yourself say that, 'subject to certain conditions,' you believe a Palestinian state is the solution. Do you really think that Labor could have been elected in 1992 had it openly said as much to a public that had been brainwashed against such an idea for years? And with whom could one negotiate such a solution *except* the PLO, an organization that Israeli voters feared and abhorred? No serious person expects politicians always to tell the truth. It is a leader's duty to get elected and lead, not to get permission for every step he takes."

Despite my own reputation among my friends as a cynic, such a view, which is almost universally held today on the Israeli Left, strikes me as cynical beyond bounds. Of course politicians frequently lie to the public, although those who lie least and with the uneasiest conscience are the ones who look best in the history books. But it is one thing to lie about ordinary matters of political expediency, another to lie about a momentous decision that will profoundly affect the future of one's country for as long as it continues to exist. If the question of Israel's borders, of their location and defensibility, of who lives and rules on either side of them, and of their relationship to the claims of thousands of years of Jewish history is not something about which to consult the Israeli public within the framework of democratic politics, what is democracy for?

Nor is it the case that Labor had to fool the voters in order to carry out its present policies. There were other alternatives. Having won the elections on the platform it ran on, Labor could have begun to prepare public opinion for the new direction it wished to take. It could have asked the PLO to help change the climate in Israel by declaring a moratorium on terror, or by repealing the provisions of the Palestinian Charter which call for Israel's destruction, or some other dramatic act. It could have begun tentative, noncommittal talks with the PLO and then revealed their content to the public. And having done any or all of these things, it could then have said:

> Citizens of Israel: now that you have seen how the PLO has changed and is ready to recognize the state of Israel and live peacefully alongside it, we are calling new elections in order to ask you for a mandate to commence negotiations with it that may lead to a Palestinian state.

Would that mandate have been given? It is impossible to say. But whether or not, the people would have spoken. And perhaps if the people had been allowed to speak, Yitzhak Rabin would be alive today.

· · · · ·

Or perhaps not? His murderer was a true believer in the Land of Israel, not in democratic procedures. Still, as has been frequently pointed out in the wake of the assassination, true believers tend to reach for their guns when they feel the rage of a wider public behind them—and the rage of many Israelis against Yitzhak Rabin dated to the day when, without asking or warning them, he signed an agreement with Yasir Arafat, a man regarded by them with revulsion, and shook hands with him on the White House lawn. Although those who in the next two years accused Rabin of betraying his country were speaking overheatedly, he did betray many of the voters whose ballots helped elect him Prime Minister by a narrow margin.

Rabin's turnabout has been compared by his defenders to that of Likud's Menachem Begin, who was elected in 1977 on a platform that never hinted he would return all of Sinai to Egypt. But there is a huge difference. When Begin submitted the accord with Egypt to the Knesset, it won overwhelming bipartisan approval, with an even higher percentage of Labor members than Likud members voting for it; had he called for new elections, he would have won them handily. By contrast, the Rabin-Arafat rapprochement split Israel in half, both in the Knesset and in the opinion polls. The Knesset's bitterly debated ratification of Stage 2 of the Oslo agreement, a month before the assassination, passed by a vote of 61 to 59. Minus the five votes of two anti-Zionist Arab parties that object to the definition of Israel as a Jewish state, the results were 59 to 56 against.

Granted, a parliamentary majority of two is as binding as one of 200. The question in Israel was never the Rabin government's formal legitimacy, it was its political and moral wisdom in pursuing a course that turned Israel ferociously against itself on a matter of the utmost historical gravity. But as Rabin followed this course, and was applauded by the same Left that in 1982 had denounced Begin's invasion of Lebanon for violating the principle that no Israeli government should go to war without a national consensus, he and his supporters scoffed at the proposition that a radically conceived peace demanded a measure of national unity, too.

Moreover, it was clear to many thinking Israelis that, even if the Rabin government had received the nation's backing to sign the accord reached at Oslo; and even if this accord led in a few years' time to a "final" peace settlement with the Palestinians, there was no certainty that its finality would be final. A Palestinian state, even one based on a complete Israeli withdrawal to the 1967 lines, would comprise only 23 percent of the area of British Mandate Palestine. It is no secret that many and probably most Palestinians, including the leaders of the PLO, hoped such a state would be the first stage in reclaiming more Palestinian land, possibly up to the 1947 partition borders and beyond.

Indeed, while it seemed obviously in Israel's interest that any Palestinian state be an economic and political success, the more successful this state was, the more Israel's own Arab citizens, of whom there are at present nearly a million largely concentrated in the Galilee, would be encouraged to want to join it. Given the current mood of disaffection toward Israeli society felt by most Israeli Arabs, whose sense of Palestinian identity has been greatly strengthened by the installation of the PLO next-door to them, a movement for *Anschluss* with the state of Palestine would be likely to develop among them in the future, plunging Israel back into a period of bitter internal Arab-Jewish strife that would probably draw into it not only an irredentist Palestine but still other Arab countries. The better the peace process went in the short run, therefore, the riskier it might turn out in the end.

Thus it was that, from the autumn of 1993 to the autumn of 1995, as the Oslo agreement was implemented and thousands of armed

Palestinian policemen arrived in Gaza and Jericho and began moving into the West Bank; and as some 150 Israelis died in Palestinian terror attacks which the PLO, while procrastinating about the Palestinian Charter, was not particularly vigilant in preventing; and as the Rabin government continued to keep secret from its own people what its aims were in the peace process, including the borders it planned to insist on and its conception of the fate of the tens of thousands of Jewish settlers living beyond them, much of Israel felt like passengers on a ship that had been hijacked by its own captain and crew, who were now piloting it through a dense fog and mined waters, with the consent of half of those aboard, toward an unrevealed and perhaps calamitous destination.

The emotions aroused by this were fear, helplessness, bitterness, frustration, and, as I have said, rage. All of them were channeled into the anti-government invective that mounted in volume and vituperation throughout this period and that was, so the Israeli Left now tells us, the finger that pressed the trigger that was Yigal Amir.

· · · · ·

I would not dispute this. Although Amir was apparently unaided on the night of the shooting, he was what is known in Hebrew as a *sh'liah avera*, a messenger of sin, for a large body of Israelis who would not have dreamed of doing what he did. This public, heavily represented in what is known as the "national-religious camp" and in the settlements of Judea and Samaria that are the most threatened by the Oslo pact, owes itself and the nation a reckoning for having allowed elements in its midst to be swept away by inflammatory rhetoric and bizarre rabbinical rulings that could have encouraged a Yigal Amir to think he was acting on its behalf

Such a reckoning, at least part of the Israeli Right is now making. The reckoning that is not being made, and of the need for which there seems to be no awareness among those who should make it, concerns the rhetoric and deeds of the Left, hardly any less inflammatory during the period in question.

Before me is the pro-government newspaper *Ha'aretz*, Israel's most respected daily, from March 26, 1995. Its front-page headline: "Rabin: Likud Is Collaborator With Hamas." The text of the lead article reports that "Prime Minister Yitzhak Rabin sharply attacked Likud yesterday [saying], 'The terror organizations are succeeding because Likud has become a collaborator with Islamic Jihad and Hamas.'" It goes on:

In inner consultations recently held at high levels of the Labor party, it was decided to step up attacks against the Right, especially against Likud and its leader. There is concern in Labor over polls, taken in the last several months, showing [Benjamin] Netanyahu with a large lead over Rabin.... Ranking members of Labor welcomed this changed line. One cabinet minister said he was happy that "The Prime Minister has decided to take off the gloves with Likud." A second minister, on the other hand, expressed concern that extreme language might cause the political arena to degenerate into verbal violence a year before the elections....

It would be interesting to know who the prescient second minister was. And it would be interesting to ask the first minister whether, if a left-wing assassin had killed Benjamin Netanyahu, he would now be saying that Yitzhak Rabin had "blood on his hands," as Labor has been saying of Netanyahu.

As it happens, Netanyahu and Likud have been specifically charged by the Left not so much with direct incitement as with failing to disown incendiary language and symbolism coming from extra-parliamentary right-wing groups—the prime example, repeatedly cited since the assassination, being the blind eye turned by them to a poster of Rabin in an SS uniform displayed by demonstrators at a Likud rally in October. This poster, it now appears, was commissioned and disseminated by Avishai Raviv, a right-wing extremist who was, however, acting as an agent for the Israeli General Security Service: i.e., the Rabin government itself

This does not exonerate the failure of the Right to react more strongly—but it is worth recalling that throughout the 1980s, long before it was employed by the right wing as a term of abuse, the word "Nazi" was often used by the far Left to describe the settlers and the Likud government that backed them. Perhaps the most egregious case was that of the late Yeshayahu Leibowitz, a well-known theologian and political polemicist, who invented the term "Judeo-Nazi" and who in 1993 was awarded the prestigious Israel Prize for intellectual achievement by Yitzhak Rabin's Minister of Culture, Shulamit Aloni. There was nothing wrong in calling Jews Nazis, it would seem, as long they were the right Jews.

Indeed, there was nothing wrong with calling the settlers many other names, too, which were routinely hurled at them by the Left in a systematic attempt to delegitimize them after they began organizing against the Oslo agreement: "enemies of peace," "religious fanatics," "dancers on the blood [of terror victims]," "Arab-haters," and

"Hamasniks" were some of the more common epithets. It made no difference that these same settlers, who for years had braved the daily dan-
gers of the *intifada,* had been, in the name of the national security of Israel,
assisted and encouraged to take up residence in their homes by previous Israeli governments, including the earlier 1974–77 regime of Yitzhak
Rabin. Asked about one of their demonstrations, the same Rabin now
declared that, for his part, "They can spin around like propellers for as
long as they like."

Another example of right-wing incitement said to have provoked
the assassination were the placards and shouts of "Rabin Is a Murderer"
at many anti-government demonstrations, especially after Palestinian
terror attacks. These were reprehensible—but the copyright on them,
too, belonged to the Left. Such slogans first surfaced in Israel in 1982, at
the huge Labor-party and Peace Now rally held in Tel Aviv's Kings of
Israel Square (now Yitzhak Rabin Square) to protest the massacre of Palestinians by Lebanese Christians in the Sabra and Shatila refugee camps.
There, signs proclaiming "Begin Is a Murderer" and "Sharon Is a Murderer" were held high by many demonstrators. I can vouch that no one
asked for their removal because I was there holding a sign myself
(although differently worded, as I recall).

But, protests the Left, there is no comparison: although we too may
have sinned with words, nearly all the threats and incidents of political
violence that Israel has witnessed in recent years have come from the
Right. This is true. Right-wing extremism in Israel *has* been more violent; one reason for this is that, ideologically, the far Right tends to view
conflict, rather than the resolution of it, as an inescapable existential
imperative of Israeli Jews. And yet the Machiavellian use, by a secret
service controlled by the Rabin government, of *agents provocateurs* like
Raviv to foment and aggravate such violence as a means of discrediting
the opposition to the peace process is no less frightening than the violence itself. Political thuggery is a grave threat to a democracy; employing a secret service to manipulate a country's political life in favor of its
ruling party, let alone by paying hoodlums to threaten and assault people and destroy property, is far graver, reminiscent of some of the most
unsavory regimes of our century.

In the end, perhaps, it is pointless to try to keep score in such a
game of tit-before-tat. Indeed, although both the Right and the Left contributed generously to the acrimonious atmosphere that was created in
the period after Oslo, it is on the whole remarkable, given the passions
aroused by one of the most agonizingly fateful moments the Jewish peo-

ple has ever lived through, that democratic forms have been so well observed in Israel up to the assassination. (Since the assassination there have been signs that the Labor government has embarked on a worrisome policy of using rarely invoked anti-"incitement-to-rebellion" laws in order to intimidate forms of protest and criticism that would be permitted, or at least considered less severe legal offenses, in most democratic countries.) In terms of the tone of the political debate, Dreyfusards and anti-Dreyfusards in France, pro- and anti-Vietnam-war demonstrators in the United States, were no more polite when arguing about much less. They, after all, were fighting only for the soul of their country; here the struggle is over the limbs of the body as well.

· · · · ·

One can point to the exact historical moment when the center dropped out of Israeli politics, leaving an overwhelmingly secular Left and a heavily religious Right facing each other across a discourseless chasm. But although this happened politically in September 1993 with the signing of the Oslo agreement, culturally it was a long while in the making.

In a deep sense, the processes leading up to this moment reflect the failure of the grand cultural project of Zionism, whose root assumption, once shared by secular and religious Zionists alike, was that it was possible to build a society that would combine a commitment to the modern world and its highest ideals with an allegiance, if not to the ritual forms, at least to the great texts and memories of Jewish tradition and their resonance in the physical landscape of Israel.

For most of this century, as reflected in literature, arts, popular culture, and politics, this project had every appearance of success. As late as the 1960s, the same Bible which, shortly before his death, Yitzhak Rabin referred to as "an antiquated land registry" was still a living book in secular Israel. Here is Moshe Dayan, a product of the Labor movement and only seven years older than Rabin, speaking a month after the Six-Day war of 1967 placed in Jewish hands the portion of central Palestine that had been lost to Jordan in the unavoidable partition of 1948:

> We have returned to the mountainland, to the cradle of our people and the legacy of our fathers, to the land of the judges and to the bastion of the kingdom of the House of David. We have returned to Hebron, to Shechem [Nablus], to Bethlehem, to Anatot, to Jericho, and to the fords of the Jordan.

Today, when such language in the mouth of a Labor-party politician would sound hopelessly archaic, it is possible to see that Dayan's generation derived its own romantic attachment to the Bible and Jewish history less (as Zionist myth had it) from the vaunted contact of the native-born *sabra* with the soil of the land of Israel than from its East-European-born parents, themselves the products of religious homes; and that the apparent link binding Hebrew secularism to Jewish tradition was perhaps less a viable carrying forward of tradition than tradition's last gasp. What has happened with the final expiration of that gasp is well illustrated by the case of Moshe Dayan's daughter Ya'el, a left-wing Labor politician whose only known public reference to the Bible, made in defense of gay rights, has been to assert that David and Jonathan were homosexual lovers, and who has declared that she will be happy to visit Hebron on a Palestinian visa.

It was the Palestinians in the occupied territories, certainly, who hastened a polarization in Israeli life that would have taken place far more slowly and less painfully without them. For as the Israeli occupation of the territories lengthened, and the Jewish settlement movement grew, and with it the increasingly organized and violent resistance of the local Palestinian population, culminating in the *intifada,* the choice became a seemingly stark one. Either Israel relinquished its title to Judea and Samaria, the geographical core of the historical Jewish homeland, and so, by freeing the people living there from its yoke, took its stand (said the Left) with enlightened humanity; or else it pressed its claim to the areas and kept faith (said the Right) with Jewish memory.

This was a cruel dilemma. And it represented a great irony, for it meant that the Jewish state, which according to Zionism had come to heal the inner split between the human being in the Jew and the Jew in the human being, had now driven a new and terrible wedge into the breach.

Like a man in great torment who breaks psychologically in two, Israel thus went, or was dragged, to Oslo as two nations, each willing to risk what the other was not and unwilling to risk what the other was; neither able to communicate with or to understand the other but only to blame the other rancorously; thesis and antithesis, each half of the now-fractured personality of the Jewish people in its homeland.

I am not a believer in the view that tormented nations need psychiatrists rather than politicians. Only a wise politics can help to join again what a foolish politics has helped to sunder. But can one, in today's circumstances, imagine a politics wise enough?

—January 1996

Nadav Haetzni

In Arafat's Kingdom

On Sunday, July 28 of this year, a young man, diagnosed as brain-dead, was hospitalized in Nablus, a city on the West Bank under the rule of Yasir Arafat's Palestinian Authority (PA). According to the Palestinian security agents who brought him in, his name was Ahmad Sabah, and he was from Jenin, another West Bank town. For some reason, no one—no family members, no friends—came to look in on him.

To the medical staff of the hospital it was clear the mortally ill young man had undergone unspeakable suffering. His skull had been crushed by repeated blows, and every inch of his body was covered with reddish or bluish bruises. The severe burns on his chest and back told of torture by means of red-hot iron bars. Although the hospital made an attempt to find out what had happened, it was unable even to trace the man's identity.

Early the next day, a directive arrived from the security forces: the patient was to be transferred to a hospital in Ramallah, another town under the PA's jurisdiction about fifteen minutes by car from Israel's capital city of Jerusalem. There he was carried into the intensive-care unit, entrance to which was barred by four men armed with Kalashnikov assault rifles. Not even Bassam Eid, a well-known Palestinian human-rights activist who had been identified as a relative of the young man, was allowed in. Only that evening did a Nablus resident who was visiting a different patient in the hospital blunder by accident into the intensive-care unit, notice the clinically dead man, and recognize his features. Soon the story was out.

57

The pseudonymous youngster from Jenin turned out to be Mahmoud Jumayel, a leader of Fatah, Yasir Arafat's own movement, in Nablus. By the time his death was officially confirmed two days later, Palestinian riots had broken out in the West Bank. For the first time in history, however, these riots were aimed not at the Israeli but at the Palestinian "occupier"—Yasir Arafat himself.

Indeed, the final months of Mahmoud Jumayel's life throw into sharp relief the contours of a new Palestinian tragedy, just as they expose a deep sickness at the heart of the fledgling administration of the PLO chairman. At the signing of the Oslo peace accords in September 1993, the highest hopes were expressed by all parties for the new era that was about to dawn in the Middle East. Not only would peaceful relations at last obtain between Israel and its oldest antagonist, the Palestinian Arabs, but those Arabs themselves, liberated from the foreign occupier's yoke, would quickly reap the benefits of self-rule and democratic rights, and be enabled at last to develop the free civic institutions guaranteed them by the charter of the PLO. Less than two and a half years later, whatever the state of relations between the PA and Israel, it is all too clear that Arafat and his henchmen have brought to the lives of their fellow Palestinians a level of brutality and corruption reminiscent of some of the Arab world's most benighted regimes.

. . . . .

Mahmoud Jumayel was not exactly an angel. As a leader of the Fatah youth movement he had taken an active role in the *intifada*, the violent uprising against Israel that began in the late 1980s. Later, during the twilight days of Israeli rule in Nablus, he prominently supported one of the most despotic local gangs (Tabuk) in its rivalry with Jibril Rajoub, head of one of the PA's notorious security agencies. So long as Israeli forces remained in Nablus, Rajoub could not prevail over his rivals; but with the accession of the PA in December 1995, Rajoub arrested Jumayel and one of his associates.

The two men were detained in a jail in Jericho. They were not interrogated, and no charges were filed. Though their distraught families knocked desperately on every door, and sent endless petitions to their esteemed leader in Gaza, no response was forthcoming; no one in a position of authority even consented to see them, and senior members of Fatah who inquired into the matter were told to mind their own business. And so Jumayel sat in prison for seven months. What happened to change things on July 27 is still not known—the PA has refused all requests for information—but upon his transfer from Jericho to Nablus,

Jumayel was handed over for some reason to investigators from the Palestinian naval command, who proceeded to string him up, crack his skull with blunt instruments, flog him with chains, and sear his flesh.

But as we have seen, the story did not end there. Apprised of what their stooges had done, PA officials compounded brutality with subterfuge, first hospitalizing their captive under a false name and then transferring him from hospital to hospital. When, finally, the truth came out, and public anger mounted, Arafat resorted—characteristically—to damage control: he announced the formation of a committee to investigate the cause of death. Whether such a committee was in fact ever formed is uncertain; if so, it investigated nothing. But, evidently alarmed by the intensity of the public protest, Arafat then undertook another characteristic initiative, convening a "state security court" in Jericho. This factitious body, composed of three military officers, conducted a hasty show trial of the officers who had tortured Mahmoud Jumayel to death. The men promptly confessed, and in the space of four hours, without benefit of substantive legal defense, they were convicted of all charges and handed lengthy prison sentences.

Scapegoats had been found, and more searching and decisive inquiries successfully avoided: who gave the order to interrogate and torture Jumayel; by whose authority had he been detained without trial for seven months, and why; who was responsible for the attempt to cover up the affair? Reporting on Jumayel's funeral, Palestinian newspapers highlighted the words of a eulogy said to have been delivered by his father over the open grave, unreservedly praising his illustrious leader Abu Amar (Arafat's *nom de guerre*). But Palestinian papers publish what the PA dictates; the fact is that shortly before the funeral procession began, Mahmoud's grieving father had spoken to reporters with exceptional harshness about Arafat. Either he was compelled under threat to deliver a prepared text at the graveside or the papers simply printed a eulogy that was never spoken.

· · · · ·

Thus the saga of Mahmoud Jumayel, as of mid-August the eighth detainee known to have been murdered by torture in a Palestinian jail. *Thousands* like him are being held behind bars without trial; thousands have been tortured; hundreds have been murdered for political reasons.

Who is behind these deeds? At the time of the Oslo agreement, the PLO command resided in Tunis, where it had ended up after long years of wandering from one Arab state to another. Arafat's troops, in particular those designated the Palestine Liberation Army (PLA), were scattered all over the Arab world—one unit in Iraq, a second in Jordan, a third in Egypt, and so forth. Enlisted men and officers, some veterans, others fresh recruits, did not exactly constitute a fighting force. Many of them had settled into the countries in which they were billeted, had taken jobs, and were merely collecting a salary from the PLO. They adhered to the norms of their adopted societies and had even begun to speak with an Iraqi or Egyptian accent.

Senior officers did not even know who their counterparts were elsewhere, or, for that matter, who was who in the PLO command structure. Inside the PLA, exaggerated attention was paid to matters of rank and hierarchy. There were stubborn rumors of corruption among officers, of mistreatment of subordinates, of cowardice in battle. Needless to say, this did not prevent anyone's advancement in the ranks; that depended on one criterion alone, namely, loyalty to the chairman.

The PLO's political officers were likewise scattered and likewise enmeshed in their local scenes, whether in Tunis, Amman, or Cairo. Educated at the feet of Arab despots, they maintained among themselves no orderly system of relationships; all lines led in one direction only, to Arafat. From grand strategy to trifles, everything began and ended with him.

Upon their entry into "liberated Palestine"—i.e., Gaza and Jericho—in May 1994, both the political officers and the PLA troops met up with and joined the top echelon of indigenous Fatah activists. There were two main criteria for appointing the latter to senior positions in the new military structures of the PA: personal closeness to the chairman, and length of stay in an Israeli prison. From the point of view of building a professional cadre, this was bad enough; much worse was what Arafat proceeded to do.

Far from attempting to transform the diverse units and their officers into a unified security force with a single hierarchy, the PLO chairman took the existing chaos and made it worse. As is well known, Arafat is congenitally suspicious of order and system, not to mention power consolidated in the hands of a hierarchy or any other center that might threaten his preeminence. In line with this, he established something like eight different security agencies with parallel and competing mandates. Though they bear impressive and comprehensive-sounding titles, they act as freewheeling militias or as gangs, each with its own detention centers and none accountable to anyone or anything, whether law court or legislative council. In effect, every ranking officer, and certainly every captain of a militia, is a king unto himself. In Gaza, even the fire-fighters maintain their own detention center, and freely arrest and imprison.

To this Turkish bazaar has been added the explosive issue of cultural difference. The population of the West Bank and Gaza spent 27 years under Israeli occupation—a lesson, among other things, in democracy. In those years it learned that even a man under "oppression" has rights. There is a law; there are avenues of public protest; and if all else fails there is a supreme court of justice. The encounter between the local graduates of Israeli-style democracy—even the Fatah members among them—and the new band of outsiders, violent, unrestrained, contaminated by Eastern ways, inevitably led to a collision.

· · · · ·

The problem could be contained as long as Arafat's forces were in control only in Gaza and Jericho. But by the end of 1995, when the second stage of the Oslo agreement was put into effect, men wearing the Palestinian uniform swarmed into the cities of Judea and Samaria—Ramallah, Nablus, Jenin, Bethlehem, and the rest—and the pot began to boil over. So far, the outsiders are prevailing.

In mid-July of this year, for example, one Nasser Masalmah arrived at his parent's house in the village of Bait Avva. One of many thousands of Palestinians who had cooperated with Israeli security forces in the years of Israel's administration of the territories, he had been given an Israeli identity card upon the accession of the PA and had moved into Israel proper. Now, coming home for a visit, he was picked up and brought in for questioning at a nearby Palestinian police station. (The interrogation was itself in violation of the Oslo accords, which forbid the arrest by Palestinians of anyone carrying an Israeli identity card; but such details have never troubled the PA.) At around 10:30 at night, Masalmah was released and made his way to his parents' house. An hour later, unknown persons burst in, raked the house with automatic weapons, and fled. One family member was wounded. Masalmah and his brother-in-law were killed on the spot.

No one took responsibility for the attack, but the trail pointed to Masalmah's interrogators from the Palestinian security organs: whoever released him no doubt also had sent the killers to deal with this man who had enjoyed good relations with Israel. And Masalmah is only one of hundreds of residents in the former territories who have been murdered on political grounds in the last two years. The victims are usually people considered to be "external" enemies, though not infrequently the passion for liquidation extends to members of rival security agencies.

Aside from such acts of deliberate violence, the last two and a half years have also claimed innumerable victims of official stupidity, light-mindedness, or a quick trigger finger. In April, Taysir A-Lozy, a twenty-three-year-old from Ramallah was returning from an outing with friends, and for some unknown reason their car was deemed "suspicious" by a Palestinian militiaman, who thereupon shot him in the head. As in the Jumayel case, the authorities next proceeded to cover their traces. Palestinian police attempted to kidnap the body from the local hospital in order to falsify the evidence, and then conjured up spurious charges against the young man and his companions, accusing them of drug-dealing, gun-running, and the like. The truth is that the militiaman responsible for the murder was simply acting in accordance with accepted norms—shoot first, ask questions later. No one investigates such incidents, and no one brings the perpetrators to justice.

· · · · ·

Which brings us in general to the subject of Palestinian justice.

In January 1995, a resident of Jericho by the name of Salman Jalayta, along with a number of his friends, was arrested and interrogated by men under Jibril Rajoub's command. After days of torture, Jalayta breathed his last; his body bore marks of treatment similar to that which would later be meted out to Mahmoud Jumayel (with minor embellishments—Jalayta's skin had been shredded by pincers). The other youngsters with him suffered similar treatment, though not to the point of death.

Jalayta and his comrades were publicly accused of having murdered a Jericho resident, a junior Hamas man, in a quarrel. (In what is by now a virtual convention, they were said to have collaborated with Israel.) They were also accused of larceny, lawlessness, and hooliganism. The charges were almost certainly false, but to this day none of them has been properly investigated, and Jalayta's associates are still behind bars; they have not seen a magistrate, or a written indictment. Only after relentless pressure from their families and human-rights activists did it emerge that in April of this year—that is, fifteen months after their imprisonment—the young men, unrepresented by counsel, had been tried by a military tribunal and convicted on the basis of a confession.

In early August, two Palestinian human-rights workers finally succeeded in getting hold of the young men's file. According to one of them, it was a fabrication through and through: all the documents it contained, including witnesses' depositions and the bill of indictment, were written in the same hand and bore the same date. Neither the indictment nor the "confessions" of the accused stipulated what had led to the events of which they were convicted. One of the convicted men, Rashid Fitiyani, managed to tell his mother how his signature had been procured: "When they got through smashing my bones and told me to sign, nothing mattered any more. I signed, and that was that."

The arrest and "trial" of the Jericho men illuminate some major features of the Palestinian system of justice. Prisoners are kept in jail for long months without trial, and sometimes without even an interrogation and without being told why they have been detained. When they are at last brought to trial, it is hardly ever clear under what provision of the law they have been charged, or why the trial is being conducted under one specific set of auspices rather than another.

In fact, there is no Palestinian law *per se.* Within the areas under the jurisdiction of the PA, at least four different systems are in place—Jordanian law, Egyptian law, British Mandatory law, and the revolutionary code adopted by the PLO in 1979—and no one knows which of them will be used when. Confusion reigns in the court system as well. For all practical purposes, civil courts can hardly be said to exist. There is a high court of appeals in Gaza, and another appellate court in Ramallah, but they compete in no clear-cut way with military or revolutionary courts whose very names are constantly changing. As for the military courts, they are mostly a kind of front, at the service of the regime when and as needed: a group of reliable officers is assembled, they set up an impromptu courtroom in some military installation or other, and hastily perform the task required of them by the chairman.

Lately a group of lawyers has turned to the appellate court in Ramallah demanding the release of ten students who have been held without a hearing since last March. The government prosecutor has responded that the appellate court lacks jurisdiction in the case. This confronts the magistrates with an exceptionally difficult dilemma. They must be well aware that if they rule against the prosecutor, not only will no one honor the ruling, but they may end up paying for their rashness. They have only to look to the example of Qusai Abdallah, chief justice of the supreme court of appeals in Gaza, who in early June dared to rule against the government prosecutor in the false arrest of the human-rights activist Eyad Sarraj. In short order the judge was forced to retire from the bench and put under house arrest.

· · · · ·

If neither the military nor the judiciary can be trusted by ordinary Palestinians, what, then, of their representative institutions, or the media?

In late January of this year, voting took place for a new Palestinian Legislative Council. Former President Jimmy Carter, on hand for the occasion, duly pronounced the election democratic to a fault, and so did an international team of observers, cheered on by an Israeli government anxious to confer the tokens of legitimacy on its peace partner. Had the elections been properly inspected, however, a different picture would have emerged: not only were they undemocratic, they were not even proper elections.

For one thing, the Islamic resistance had condemned the exercise from the outset and for the most part refused to participate. For another, Arafat saw to it through the usual means that dissenting candidates would not be elected in any significant number, and he also winnowed his own Fatah list to make sure it was filled with yes-men. Here and there, it is true, he faced opposition—honest and brave men and women— but in general he was able to ensure himself a sweeping victory. The majority of those elected were drawn from the innards of his political apparatus.

The vote produced a council of 88 members whose job is to serve as a legislative assembly—a parliament, for all intents and purposes— but there can be no illusion that this parliament has teeth. It cannot influence, it cannot criticize, and it has not legislated a single matter of substance. Arafat freely ignores any action of which he does not approve, including the five proposals put forward so far for a proper constitution. At the end of July, when the subject of the constitution was about to be broached yet again, the chairman turned to the members, denounced them as "sons of whores"—and left the chamber. Whereupon the deliberations ended.

As for the administrative functions of government, though Arafat committed himself at Oslo to forming proper institutions—offices and ministries with orderly tables of organization, a professional bureaucracy, agreed-upon procedures for decision-making—no real thought was ever given to the matter, and from the start the executive institutions of the PA were staffed mostly with Arafat loyalists. A handful of Palestinian intellectuals, educated in Western universities, could be heard warning that a decade's imprisonment, or family ties to a given cabinet minister, or for that matter fanatic loyalty to Yasir Arafat himself did not necessarily constitute qualification for public office; what was needed were trained professionals, expertise, objective norms and standards. Nobody took the warnings seriously, and the results are evident for all to see.

Then there are the Palestinian press and broadcast media, an area in which Arafat's hand is especially evident. Most Palestinian papers of any substance are printed and published in the relatively protected environs of Jerusalem, the capital of the Zionist state. Yet despite this fact, and despite the shining model afforded by the unfettered Israeli press right next door, the PA has managed over the last year and a half to terrorize virtually every Palestinian publisher, editor, and journalist and turn him into a faithful parrot of the Arafat line.

Practically immediately upon the entry of the PA into Gaza and Jericho in mid-1994, for example, Arafat issued an order to close *Al-Nahar,* a daily newspaper which he accused of serving as a mouthpiece for King Hussein of Jordan. The paper's publisher, although he lived and worked in Jerusalem, did not dare defy the order from Gaza. Within 40 days of the shut-down, thoroughly broken, he agreed to accept Arafat's dictates and *Al-Nahar* began to appear again, as a now-dependable adherent of the "Palestinian national line."

In the days and months following, other editors and reporters received the personal attentions of Arafat's men whenever they dared write or publish something displeasing to the regime. One such incident occurred eighteen months ago, when a number of papers made the mistake of reporting the exact size of a rally held by the opposition. Summoned to a meeting, the editors were officially informed that henceforth they were authorized to publish only those texts and statistics given to them by Wafa, the Palestinian news service. Those failing to knuckle under, like the opposition paper *Al-Ummah,* were physically attacked: Arafat's security forces first confiscated the newspaper's press plates and then burned down its offices, which again were located in Jerusalem. (The Rabin government, which knew all about the incident, said nothing.)

These various actions had the desired effect, especially when combined with arrests. A journalist named Samir Hamatu, apparently suspected of having links to the Islamic opposition, has been sitting in jail in Gaza since March, unindicted and untried. Another, the night editor of *Al-Quds,* the largest Palestinian daily, having flouted an order from Gaza to headline some flattering remarks about Arafat uttered by a Christian patriarch, was kidnapped—yet again within Jerusalem—and held in prison for five days in Jericho until he learned his lesson.

On the radio, the "Voice of Palestine" has been docile from the start. Nevertheless, the station's most popular broadcaster, Danial Karim Halaf, was fired after she permitted a critic of the regime to express his views on the air.

· · · · ·

Helping to keep the PA enterprise afloat are corruption and graft, both petty and large-scale. On the level of the petty, which is what most Palestinians see every day, the practice among many PA officials is to help themselves to goods and services: when, for instance, the commander of one of the many security agencies operating in Bethlehem wants a haircut, his men block off the street and allow no one to pass until their chieftain has been served (gratis, naturally).

An intricate system of localized gangsterism and patronage has also sprung up. A resident of a village near Ramallah found himself in jail after accidentally hitting a car belonging to the son of a Palestinian cabinet minister; another resident, an engineer by profession, got two broken ribs after he declined to vacate the parking spot of the same minister's wife. On the other hand, if a local is lucky enough to have friends in high places, not even the legal rights of another Palestinian will hinder him from getting his way. Thus, in the Christian town of Beit Jallah south of Jerusalem, a woman fell out with two of her neighbors over a plot of land. Though the neighbors were from an important local family, and were in the legal right, the woman had an advantage: connections with the local police chief. Her adversaries were promptly seized and tortured until they agreed to sign away their claim to the disputed property.

As in most societies, events on the local level give a hint of arrangements at the top—in this case, the wholesale economic swindling of foreign donors and others by the PA elite.

In October 1993, at the height of the Oslo euphoria, a group of countries led by the U.S. agreed to contribute a total of $2.1 billion to the PA over a period of five years, as a token of support for the young democracy-in-the-making. Various conditions were attached to the gift, among them the establishment of an agency that would be responsible for absorbing and distributing the funds in accordance with strict accounting procedures. This agency was indeed set up, under the name Palestinian Economic Council for Development and Reconstruction (PECDAR). But the donor nations, instead of being rewarded with oversight and integrity in the handling of their money, have been treated to duplicity and obfuscation.

PECDAR was supposed to be wholly independent of the PA; its mandate was to ensure that the sums coming from abroad would flow especially to development projects. Today, the agency is entirely in the hands of Arafat, and most of the money that has already been contributed has gone not to development projects but to the establishment and maintenance of a growing military machine and a swollen government bureaucracy. At the same time, an impressive portion of the money—the gift of European and, especially, American taxpayers—has ended up in the pockets of senior PA officials. Arafat himself and his closest associates skim from the top, the former to subsidize his political activities, the latter to fatten their personal bank accounts.

It is not just foreign governments that are being ripped off. Private investors contemplating doing business under the PA can likewise expect to forgo hefty sums in graft and hush money. Muhammad Rashid, Arafat's economic adviser, is among those benefiting financially from every sack of cement, every carton of cigarettes, that comes into Gaza. One consequence of all this activity has been a marked rise in the quality of motor transport among PA officials. The astonishing number of luxuriously appointed Mercedeses adorning the streets of Gaza and the West Bank stands in stark contrast to the steadily shrinking economic prospects of ordinary Palestinians, many of whom—thanks to the failure or refusal of Arafat to curb terrorism against Israel—have been cut off from their source of livelihood by a closure of the territories and are on the brink of starvation. As the plight of the average Palestinian in the autonomous region worsens, the wealth of the PA political elite grows ever more conspicuous.

· · · · ·

How long can this go on? Lately, indeed, it has become possible to gauge the degree of dissatisfaction with Arafat's rule on the part of his subjects. In early August, as I noted above, popular riots broke out in two Palestinian towns, Nablus and Tulkarm. In Tulkarm, a mob of thousands gathered. Before things got out of hand, the angry crowd pulled down a giant poster of Arafat that hung in the town square (it had been paid for, under coercion, by a local publisher) and tore it to shreds. In the melee, some 50 to 60 detainees broke out of prison and managed to get away before police began shooting, killing one demonstrator.

This was six weeks after Benjamin Netanyahu's upset victory in the Israeli elections, an event that was greeted, ironically enough, by jubilation among many Arabs in Hebron and East Jerusalem, two

Palestinian strongholds which have yet to fall to the tender mercies of the PA. Some were open in expressing their joy; others whispered the hope that the new Israeli Prime Minister would yet rescue them from the clutches of dictatorship.

Around the same time, the lines outside the branch of the Israeli office of internal affairs in East Jerusalem began to lengthen. Most of the people there were anxious to apply, at any price, for an Israeli identity card. Throughout the PA, indeed, this blue card has become the most desirable commodity imaginable—a ticket out of hell.

But relatively few will receive a blue identity card, and relatively few will be able to save themselves. What then? Although the full scope of what is going on in the areas under the jurisdiction of the PA may not be known to the Western public, there is no doubt that interested Western governments have been apprised of every detail, and (like at least the previous Israeli government) have sedulously maintained silence. That silence is perhaps best explained by an offhand remark of the late Yitzhak Rabin, who once expressed his confidence in Yasir Arafat's ability to deal handily with his internal opposition, unhampered (in contrast to Rabin himself) by "the [Israeli] Supreme Court and [the Israeli human-rights organization] B'Tselem."

Rabin, in truth, had little interest in the human rights of Palestinians. What he cared about was the continuation of the political process initiated with Arafat at Oslo. So, too, the present administration in Washington; so, too, the donor nations of Western Europe; and so, too, those Arab countries which have declared their political support of the PA (Arab financial support has been minimal). Any effort to rein in this tyranny, to encourage the formation of real democratic institutions and a society of law, would have to come from those in possession of a stick—namely, the donors, and especially the U.S. Such an effort would bring untold benefits to the Palestinian people; but it would also clearly endanger the man, and the men, at the top. So far, and no doubt for that very reason, there is not the slightest sign of its happening.

—October 1996

Yuval Steinitz

When the Palestinian Army Invades

Whatever they may have accomplished or failed to accomplish politically, the Oslo accords of 1993 between Israel and Yasir Arafat's Palestine Liberation Organization have transformed Israel's security situation in ways that have still not been squarely faced. Much of the territory in the West Bank and Gaza that Israel occupied in the 1967 Six-Day war is now governed by the Palestinian Authority (PA). This embryonic state already possesses a large, militia-like police force comprising some 40,000 men; depending upon the outcome of present negotiations, it may come to acquire a combination of paramilitary and military forces as well. Although Israel will undoubtedly retain military superiority over its fledgling Arab neighbor, the threat that neighbor poses in combination with the rest of the Arab world is already significant, and is certain to grow with time.

·　·　·　·　·

Despite its obvious strategic strengths, Israel has chronically suffered from two Achilles' heels that make its defeat militarily thinkable. The first is demographic. Israel's minuscule population, combined with the sensitivity of Israeli society to the loss of life, casts a giant shadow of doubt over the country's ability to withstand an extended conventional war with the surrounding Arab world. If its enemies could force upon it a conflict lasting months or years, they would significantly improve their chances of prevailing. The Israeli response to this longstanding problem has been to accelerate the moment of cease-fire by rapidly

69

transferring the battleground to enemy territory and/or attacking the enemy's infrastructure by means of air power.

Of much greater importance, however, is the second Achilles' heel, which is geographic. The tiny area of the Jewish state, together with its overreliance on reserve forces (itself partly a product of the country's demographic weakness), casts a giant shadow of doubt of another kind altogether: namely, over its ability to withstand a *lightning* strike. An enemy's penetration into the heart of Israel could prevent the mobilization and equipment of its military reserves in addition to interrupting many other vital operations. To this second problem the traditional Israeli response has been a very fast system of mobilization—since the 1973 Yom Kippur war, the entire procedure has been designed to take no more than 24 hours—plus the reliance on superior air power to abort an enemy's attack on the first day of battle.

This is where Oslo comes in: the influx of Palestinian forces into Israel's center has greatly exacerbated the problem presented by the country's second Achilles' heel, to the extent that a total collapse of the overall strategic balance is now possible.

How so? The approximately 40,000 policemen now at the disposal of Arafat are already organized into a semimilitary structure. They are known to have some 30,000 automatic weapons in their arsenal, along with a significant number of machine guns, light antitank missiles, grenades and rocket-propelled grenades, land mines and explosives. They may also have, or be able surreptitiously to obtain from Arab countries, more advanced weapons, including handheld Strela and Stinger surface-to-air missiles. Obviously, these forces are not going to defeat the armed might of Israel in battle. But if, even as currently constituted, they were to be deployed in a coordinated fashion in the opening phases of a broader Arab assault, they could wreak havoc of a decisive kind.

A good portion of the Palestinian police is installed in the towns of Qalkilya, Tulkarm, Bethlehem, Ramallah, and Jenin on the West Bank— in other words, in areas adjacent to Israel's most vulnerable sectors, military and civilian alike. These nerve centers of Israel's life could be successfully infiltrated by a mere 10 percent of the Palestinian police force, thus transforming them into a crucial front in a comprehensive regional conflagration.

Crossing Israel's 1967 borders in small fighting units of ten to twenty men, these 4,000 men could make their way in civilian vehicles along a labyrinthine network of roads and paths with which they are intimately familiar. They would need no more than an hour to reach extremely sensitive points in the heart of Israel. Once there, they could wholly subvert the 24-hour mobilization strategy Israel relies on to fend off the far larger armies of its Arab adversaries.

If Israel were still at the initial stages of an alert, the enormous numbers of its as-yet-unarmed reservists streaming to arms depots and mobilization points would form attractive prey. Gaining control of key intersections or other advantageous locations, the Palestinian guerrilla units would be in a position to create chaos on the roads that serve as the primary arteries of mobilization and, in all probability, to kill large numbers of would-be fighters. They could also attack some of the mobilization centers themselves, most of which are not only within easy striking distance of the West Bank but also lightly guarded.

The damage that can be inflicted by small units operating against the vulnerabilities of a larger and more powerful adversary is not a matter of speculation. Among the wealth of cases that one could cite, some are from Israel's own military past. During the 1982 war in Lebanon, for example, a few dozen young, untrained Palestinian fighters armed with rocket-propelled grenades operating from hills and orchards proved far more effective in delaying Israeli traffic on a vital military highway than batteries of cannons and Katyusha rockets launched from a distance. If mini-units of this kind can succeed against heavily armored columns, how much more damage could they inflict on buses and cars filled with unarmed reservists making their way to equipment depots?

· · · · ·

Nor do key thoroughfares, intersections, and mobilization centers exhaust the list of possible targets. In all of its wars, Israel has depended heavily on the ability of its air force to gain mastery of the skies at the outset. But most Israeli air bases are quite exposed to guerrilla attack, being located within 20 to 40 kilometers of Palestinian territory. British commando operations in World War II are testimony to how easily an enemy can penetrate such installations. Leading small teams of men, Colonel David Starling of the Special Air Service successfully destroyed 250 German warplanes parked on the runways of military airfields located many kilometers behind Rommel's front lines on the North African front.

Palestinian soldiers need not actually penetrate air bases, as Starling did, to achieve their goal. Lying hidden in the foliage of orchards or farmlands outside an airfield's perimeter fence, they could employ light mortars or handheld anti-tank or surface-to-air missiles to strike Israeli planes. In previous conflicts, the Arabs have never been able to counter

Israel's superiority in the air; a surprise ground attack on its planes would thus undoubtedly present an appealing option to Arab war planners.

Finally, targeting the military is not the only means by which a broad series of Palestinian commando attacks could contribute to an effective Arab assault. Terrorist raids on residential neighborhoods or the seizure of national television and radio stations might serve to promote widespread demoralization and civilian flight. Another set of potential objectives consists of technical installations: the electric-power plant in Hadera, the oil refineries of Haifa, the chemical tanks of Gelilot, or the switchboards, transformers, and distribution boxes of the Bezek national telephone company. Power outages, huge blazes near Israel's large cities, and temporary interruptions of communication lines would all serve to paralyze if not cripple Israel in the early phases of a war.

·　·　·　·　·

Are there no effective counters to the peril posed by the armed Palestinian police? Of course there are, at least in theory. For example, Israel could fortify its border with the Palestinian Authority in particularly vulnerable sectors. It could also draw upon reserve soldiers on kibbutzim to establish lightly-armed, mobile patrol teams designed for immediate intervention in any threatened locality. Alternatively, several thousand infantry soldiers could be transferred from fighting units and assigned to a light militia scattered at different points in the Israeli rear.

Whether such measures would work if put to the test is another question. But that aside, there is, in fact, little evidence that Israel's military or political planners are giving serious attention to this or any other aspect of the ongoing transformation of the county's security position.

A number of factors are at work here. For one thing, Israeli military officials, focusing on the extreme relative weakness of the Palestinian forces and the fact that an operation involving dozens of separate guerrilla units against Israel has never been attempted, simply discount the possibility of a synchronized assault. For another, they appear to believe that Israeli intelligence would definitely enjoy between 12 and 24 hours' warning in advance of any large-scale attack, an interval sufficient to seal the borders. And even if a limited incursion were to occur, they argue, attack helicopters could provide sufficient defense for border areas.

These are all questionable assumptions. History seldom serves as a certain guide to future behavior, and to rely inflexibly on precedents is to set oneself up for a shock. It is especially foolish to depend on fixed notions of warning time: Israel's worst military fiasco occurred when it was caught unprepared by the Egyptian attack in October 1973.

Besides, it is not inconceivable that a future Palestinian government, in coordination with the major Arab states, would opt to invade with almost no advance field preparations, in a kind of "get-in, go-shoot" operation wherein commando teams would be dispatched into battle with only an hour or two of notice. This would not only achieve the element of surprise but likely increase the number of Palestinian saboteurs who could be infiltrated. Finally, since these infiltrators would need to traverse but a very short distance before being in a position to wreak major harm, and since any battles that ensued would be taking place in heavily populated areas, attack helicopters would be next to useless, if not calamitous, as a means of response.

Perhaps the most dubious supposition of all, however, is one now being bruited about in Israeli political circles. This is that the Palestinian leadership would itself be reluctant to see a decisive Arab victory over Israel, out of fear that the new Palestinian political entity would then inevitably slip under the control of either Egypt or Syria, two military giants with claims on Palestinian/Israeli territory. Since, in other words, the Palestinians have a vested interest in Israel's survival, they would not participate in any such operation. But this line of thinking is speculative in the extreme, and the very fact that it is seriously on offer suggests how eager many Israelis have become to avoid facing the still very menacing realities of the Middle East.

One does not have to go far back into the past for an example of a much greater degree of realism. Here are the words of Shimon Peres in 1978:

> The influx of a Palestinian fighting force (more than 25,000 armed fighters) into Judea and Samaria [would signify] ... an excellent starting point for mobile forces to advance immediately toward the infrastructure vital to Israel's existence.

Even after he negotiated the Oslo accords, Peres did not alter his gloomy estimation. As he argued in *The New Middle East* (1993), the situation created by an armed Palestinian state would be

> strategically fraught with catastrophe: the [country's] narrow "waist" will be susceptible to collapse by a well-organized surprise attack.... Even if the Palestinians agree to demobilize their state from both army and weapons, who can guarantee Israel that after a certain amount of time an army will not be formed, despite the agreement, which will camp at the gates of Jerusalem and the approaches of the coastal plain, and pose a substantive threat to Israel's security?

This, indeed, was the ground of Peres's opposition to the establishment of a Palestinian state. Yet what was self-evident a mere six years ago to Israel's most determined advocate of negotiations with the Palestinians is now being dismissed in the rush to conclude the "peace process."

· · · · ·

Almost 2,500 years ago, according to Thucydides, the Greek statesman Themistocles succeeded in persuading his fellow Athenians to transform their city-state into a naval power. Yet despite the vast strategic superiority it thus acquired, Athens still remained vulnerable to a simple, surprise ground attack from Sparta. In order to protect and ensure access to its new strategic assets—that is, its advanced navy and port facilities—Themistocles advocated linking the city of Athens to its port at Piraeus by means of two parallel walls.

Like ancient Athens, Israel enjoys strategic superiority over its neighbors, primarily in the realm of aeronautics and technology. Over the decades, whenever armed hostilities have broken out, this advantage has permitted Israel to strike at its enemies' rear in a manner that has eventually led to victory at the front. After 1967, Israel also enjoyed its own "walls of Themistocles," in the form of the geographic expanses of Sinai, the Golan Heights, and the West Bank. These double walls are what enabled Israel to survive the successful surprise Egyptian-Syrian attack that opened the 1973 Yom Kippur war but that was neither penetrating enough nor quick enough to take control of Israel's "Piraeus"— its airports, its reserve bases, and the like.

The deployment of light Palestinian forces throughout the West Bank has already collapsed Israel's eastern "wall" of mountains and the Jordan River, neutralizing their vital function of protecting against a sudden lightning strike aimed at the country's soft eastern flank. Indeed, if we were to consult Themistocles, he would assuredly advise us that the current Israeli defense posture is absurd. On the one hand, the state invests billions of dollars in building a modern army; purchasing state-of-the-art warplanes and constructing modern airfields; equipping and training reserve battalions; and deploying Arrow missiles. All this is right and proper and necessary. But on the other hand, it has permitted a situation to develop in which these selfsame modern, expensive systems are liable to be rendered irrelevant. On the basis of such wishful thinking, battles, and wars, are lost.

—*December 1999*

Daniel Pipes

Israel's Moment of Truth

I t might appear that things have never been going better for Israel, or worse for those who wish it ill.

Consider: the Jewish state has signed peace treaties with Egypt and Jordan, and five agreements with the Palestinian Authority (PA), its "partner for peace." With Syria, high-level negotiations now under way appear so promising that both sides have publicly predicted they could be wrapped up within a few months. Other diplomatic ties are stronger than ever: Israel has a powerful regional ally in Turkey, enjoys growing links to such giants as India and China, and is generally shedding the near-pariah status that hobbled it in the recent past. The connection to the United States is warm, deep, personal, and reciprocal.

Should diplomacy fail for any reason, moreover, Israel can fall back on its military strength. As the only country in the Middle East participating in the much-bruited "revolution in military affairs"—essentially, the application of high-tech to armaments—it has built so great a lead in conventional arms, including planes and tanks, that several Arab states have basically conceded they cannot compete with it on that level. Instead, they have directed their attention higher (to weapons of mass destruction) and lower (to terrorism). But even in those arenas, Israel is far from helpless: it has a missile-defense system, the Arrow, in the works and, for deterrent purposes, weapons of mass destruction of its own, as well as formidable anti-terrorist capabilities.

Security matters hardly exhaust the list of Israel's advantages. Economically, it enjoys today a per-capita income of $18,000, placing it a bit ahead of Spain and a bit behind Canada—in other words, in the big leagues. Better yet, it has shown a very impressive annual growth rate since 1990. Thanks to its "Silicon Wadi," Israel is a high-tech giant, with a computer and Internet sector larger in absolute terms than that of any other country in the world outside the United States. Demographically, the birth rate of 2.6 children per woman among Israeli Jews is one of the highest in the West, and the country also remains a magnet for immigration; with 5 million Jews, it is quickly gaining on the United States as the place with the largest Jewish population in the world.

Finally, there is the political scene. Unlike its neighbors and rivals, Israel benefits from a lively and robust civic culture in which everyone has his say, party lines are (notoriously) fluid, and no one defers to politicians. And yet, however colorful and argumentative the public forum, when it comes to key security issues the major parties find much common ground. In last year's elections, for example, the two candidates for the post of prime minister, Ehud Barak and Benjamin Netanyahu, differed on the tone and pace but hardly at all on the substance of the peace process: yes, they concurred, the Palestinians should do more to live up to their promises, but no, their failings in this area were not reason enough to cut off negotiations.

· · · · ·

By contrast, Arabs—and Iran, too—seem to be faring less well. Arab countries are, in the words of a UN official, "particularly exceptional in being the highest spenders in the world on military purposes": they devote 8.8 percent of their GDP to the military, versus 2.4 percent for the world as a whole. Nevertheless, despite all this spending, Arab conventional forces are in decline. To be sure, a few states (like Egypt) have access to advanced American arms, but their lack of technical proficiency means that they are nearly always consumers and not producers of military hardware, paying for completed goods that others have to teach them how to operate.

Allies? The Soviet Union is gone, and no one has come close to replacing it. The Arab states darkly suspect the United States of engaging in conspiracies against them, and these suspicions—as, most recently, in the case of the crash of an EgyptAir flight off Massachusetts—impede closer relations with the world's only superpower. Arabs also lack an effective counterpunch to the pro-Israel lobby in Washington, and have failed to respond to the growing cooperation between Turkey and Israel in a way that would advance their own interests.

Outside Israel, the Middle East boasts—if that is the right word—the world's highest quotient of autocratic regimes, not to mention an inordinate number of rogue states, including Iran, Iraq, Syria, Sudan, and Libya. A culture of deference and intimidation remains dominant everywhere; movements for democracy and human rights are feeble. Arab states are particularly vulnerable to Islamism, a totalitarian ideology in the tradition of fascism and Marxism-Leninism. While Islamists have suffered reverses in recent years, they are still the major opposition force in countries like Algeria, Egypt, and Saudi Arabia, threatening the stability of government after government.

Nor are Arab economies doing well. The recent jump in oil prices, however welcome to producers, cannot obscure some dismal realities, principally a per-capita annual income among Arabic-speaking peoples that does not rise to one-tenth of Israel's. Yes, Kuwait weighs in (just like Israel) at $18,000; but in Yemen the annual per-capita income is $270; more to the point, Egypt, Jordan, and Syria all hover in the neighborhood of $1,000. A paltry 1 percent of world equity flowing to emerging markets these days ends up in Arabic-speaking countries. When it comes to high technology, the Middle East is a black hole, with few sales and even less innovation. As the historian R. Stephen Humphreys has noted, "with the partial exception of Turkey and of course Israel . . . there is not one Middle Eastern manufactured item that can be sold competitively on world markets."

Demographically, the Arabs and Iran have too much of a good thing: a birth rate so high that schools cannot maintain standards, and economies cannot manufacture enough jobs. The demographer Onn Winckler has named population growth as the Middle East's "most critical socioeconomic problem."

Taken together, all these factors seem to suggest that Israel has at long last achieved a definitive edge over its historic enemies. Such, indeed, appears to be the view of Israeli leaders themselves. Thanks to Israel's position of strength, Prime Minister Ehud Barak now speaks confidently of an "end to wars" and of his country's being finally accepted as a permanent presence by its neighbors. These sentiments are widely echoed both in Israel and in Washington.

And yet—two trends suggest otherwise. The first has to do with Arab strengths, the second with Israeli weaknesses. In both cases, the phenomena I will be discussing are only partly material in nature, lying more in the realm of such elusive and intangible qualities as internal spirit and morale. But these are precisely the qualities that in the end can decide the fates of nations and peoples.

. . . . .

Some improvements in the Arab position, whether actual or imminent, have long been recognized: greater control over a huge portion of the world's oil and gas reserves, steady acquisition of weapons of mass destruction, movement toward economic modernization (notably in Egypt). Progress in any or all of these areas can seriously threaten Israel's qualitative edge and its security in the medium term—unless, of course, Arab enmity toward the Jewish state has dissipated in the interim. But just here is where the greatest reason for concern resides.

Historically, Arab "rejectionism"—that is, the refusal to accept the permanent existence of a sovereign Jewish state in its historic home-land—has been based on one or another local variant (pan-Arab, pan-Syrian, Palestinian, or the like) of nationalism, a European import into the Middle East. It has suffered from two disabilities: limited reach and factionalism. But in recent years, as the rejection of Israel has taken on a less secular and more Islamic complexion, it has also gained a deeper resonance among ordinary Arabs, with Israel's existence now cast as an affront to God's will, and has also benefited operationally from a some-what greater degree of unity (Islamists are surprisingly good at work-ing together). The net effect has been not to moderate but, on the con-trary, to solidify and to sharpen Arab antagonism to Israel—vocal rejectionist elements now include pious Muslims and Islamists, Arab nationalists, despots, and intellectuals—and to give fresh impetus to the dream of destroying it.

The point cannot be made often or strongly enough that, in their great majority, Arabic speakers do continue to repudiate the idea of peace with Israel.* Despite having lost six rounds of war, they seem nothing loath to try again. In one of the most recent in-depth surveys of Arab opinion, conducted by the political scientist Hilal Khashan of the Amer-ican University of Beirut, 1,600 respondents, divided equally among Jor-danians, Lebanese, Palestinians, and Syrians, stated by a ratio of 69 to 28 percent that they personally did not want peace with Israel. By 79 to 18 percent, they rejected the idea of doing business with Israelis even after a total peace. By 80 to 19 percent, they rejected learning about Israel. By 87 to 13 percent, they supported attacks by Islamic groups against Israel.

---

*For details, see my article "On Arab Rejectionism," *Commentary*, December 1997.

This is the view of Israel that dominates political debate in the Arab world and that is conveyed to the public in every arena from scholarly discourse to the popular media to nursery-school jingles. True, some Arabs think otherwise. The late King Hussein of Jordan spoke eloquently of the need to put aside the conflict with Israel and to get on with things; his son and successor appears to be of like mind. Some Arab army officers would undoubtedly prefer not to confront Israel's military forces any time soon. Kuwaitis and Lebanese Christians, sobered by occupation, now mostly wish to leave Israel alone. And there are business leaders who believe, as one Arab banker succinctly put it, that "the whole purpose of peace is business." But these elements, overall, represent but a minority of the Arab population, and have not shifted the underlying hostility.

An incident from the sports pages makes the point. Only a few months ago, Israeli athletes ventured on a first-ever official match to an Arab capital—the capital not of a front-line "confrontation state" but of the tiny and moderate Persian Gulf sheikhdom of Qatar. The experience turned out to be, as Agence France-Presse aptly characterized it, "a bruising ordeal." Forced to live in nearly complete isolation from other athletes, the Israeli champions had to enter and leave their hotel via a side door. Among the flags of the competing nations, Israel's alone was not raised in public. Huge crowds turned up to jeer at the Jewish athletes, and the media touted their presence as "an occasion to express the Arabs' rejection of all that is Israeli."

Twenty years of relations between Egypt and Israel since the treaty of 1979 testify bitterly to the same state of affairs. Formally there is peace, but Cairo permits, even sponsors, a vicious propaganda campaign against Israel that includes the crudest forms of anti-Semitism, and it is rapidly building up offensive military forces that could be deployed against the Jewish state. In effect, what Egyptian authorities are telling their people is this: for all sorts of reasons we have to be in contact with Israelis and sign certain pieces of paper, but we still hate them, and you should, too. In Jordan, where the government does not play this double game, things are in some ways worse: the best efforts of two kings have failed to induce in the Jordanian populace a more peaceable and friendly outlook toward Israel.

· · · · ·

Fueling the dream of Arab rejectionists is the immensely important fact that within Israel itself (that is, within the old 1967 borders), the Jewish proportion of the population has fallen from a one-time high of 87 percent to 79 percent today, and is inexorably trailing downward. In 1998, of Israel's total population growth of 133,000, only 80,000 were Jews, with Arabs making up the bulk of the remainder. From such statistics, some demographers predict a non-Jewish majority in Israel by the middle of the 21st century.

But the Jewish nature of the "Jewish state" will shift in the Arabs' favor long before they reach majority status there. At present, were Israeli Arabs to be represented in the Knesset in proportion to their numbers, they would already hold 24 out of its 120 seats. Even with the seven seats they now occupy, as the analyst Eric Rozenman has noted,

> the Arab electorate and Arab Knesset members ... have helped override Jewish majorities on such vital matters as the creation of Prime Minister Yitzhak Rabin's coalition in 1992 and approval of the Oslo and Oslo II accords in 1993 and 1995 respectively. All seven Israeli Arab members voted for both agreements; the former passed 61 to 50, with nine abstentions, the latter passed 61 to 59.

These trends will undoubtedly persist, Rozenman writes, especially as Israeli Arabs become "energized by a new Palestinian state next door (and perhaps also by an increasingly Palestinian Jordan)." By the time the numbers of Arabs approach or even exceed parity with the Jews, "the state might still be democratic, but the civic atmosphere, the public culture, would not likely be Jewish in the tacit, general sense it is today."

The growing power and enfranchisement of Muslims in the United States provide further grounds for Arab optimism. Not only is the American Muslim community approaching the Jewish community in absolute size, it is also making strides in education, economic well-being, and political savvy. If the old pro-Arab lobby was hampered by its dependence on oil money, retired American diplomats, and left-wing Christian Arabs, dynamic new organizations like the American Muslim Council and the Council on American-Islamic Relations are another matter altogether. Although foreign policy is hardly their only cause, "Palestine" remains the single most mobilizing issue for American Muslims, and the position articulated by Muslim organizations on this issue is almost uniformly extremist—against negotiations with Israel or accommodation with it in almost any form.

Not only are these extremist Muslim organizations intent on making themselves heard, but the Clinton administration, at least, has openly welcomed them at the highest levels. At a dinner she hosted to break the fast of Ramadan this past December, Secretary of State Madeleine K. Albright told her guests: "I want to be sure that the legitimate concerns of Muslim-Americans are taken into account when shaping the programs, activities, and reports of this Department." Seated before her was a Who's Who of American Muslim radicals.

Is it any wonder that many Arabs, knowing such facts, or hearing such heady words from the lips of the American Secretary of State, should become newly imbued with a sense of confidence about the future? And that sense can only be bolstered by what they see happening on the other side, within Israel itself.

· · · · ·

Once renowned for its self-confidence, bravery, and purpose, Israel today is a changed society. Whatever the undoubted strength of its military machine, few in a position to know the heart and soul of the country try to hide the fact of a widespread demoralization, even within that military machine itself. As a retired colonel summed it up neatly, "the Israeli public is really tired of war."

Fatigue takes many forms in contemporary Israel. The pervasive feeling that they have fought long enough, and that the time has come to settle, leads many to express openly their annoyance with the need for military preparedness and the huge expense of maintaining a modern armed force. They weary of the constant loss of life, they want escape from the fear that terrorism imparts, they yearn to close down an atavistic tribal war—and peace treaties promise a quick way out. (As one Israeli put it to me, "My grandfather, father, myself, and my son have all fought the Arabs; I want to make sure my grandson does not also have to.") Among young people, draft evasion, hitherto all but unknown, has become a serious problem, and within the army itself, morale is hardly what it once was, as the IDF's decidedly unheroic recent record in Lebanon has revealed to all, including the Hezbollah enemy.

At the same time, Israel's soaring economy has given many citizens a taste for the good life that cannot be easily reconciled with the need for patience and fortitude—and, especially, sacrifice—in confronting a seemingly unchanging enemy. Middle-aged Israeli men are increasingly unwilling to go off and "play soldier" on reserve duty for several weeks a year when they could be at the office increasing their net worth or enjoying what that net worth makes possible. For those with an active social conscience, a number of long-deferred domestic problems—

persistent poverty, a faulty educational system, worsening relations between secular and religious—seem much more deserving of attention, and of state expenditure, than does grappling endlessly with Israel's opponents.

Finally, Israelis are tired of the moral opprobrium their country has long suffered—at the United Nations, in Western academic circles, and in editorial boardrooms. Indeed, in an extreme reaction to this ongoing moral ostracism, some of the country's foremost intellectuals have, as it were, defected: they have accommodated sizable chunks of the Arab side's version of the Arab-Israeli conflict, promulgating them as important new truths. Thus, to cite an especially influential expression of this line of thinking, the school of "new historians" in Israel argues that the Jewish state is guilty of an "original sin"—the alleged dispossession of Palestine's native inhabitants—and can therefore be considered to some extent illegitimate. Others, known as "post-Zionists," have characterized Jewish nationalism—Zionism—as, if not racist, then at best an outdated and parochial ideology, and one which should no longer form the basis of Israel's public life.

Such ideas, first incubated on the far Left and in the prestige universities, then spreading to students, artists, and journalists, are now the stuff of television documentaries and educational textbooks. As of the current Israeli school year, ninth graders no longer learn that Israel's war of independence in 1948–49 was a battle of the few against the many but, to the contrary, that the Jews enjoyed military superiority over the Arabs. They also learn that many Palestinians fled the country in those war years not to clear the way for invading Arab armies thought to be on their march to victory, but out of well-founded fears of Jewish brutality and terror.

In a front-page report on the introduction of these books into the schools, the *New York Times* rightly characterized them as marking a "quiet revolution." That revolution has by now reached the consciousness of politicians, business leaders, and even military officers; its impact can hardly be exaggerated. Thanks to the inroads of post-Zionism, as Meyrav Wurmser has observed in the *Middle East Quarterly*, Israeli society "is now facing a crisis of identity and values that strikes at the basic components and elements of [its] identity: Judaism and nationalism." Without those two components, clearly, little remains of the Zionist project.

· · · · ·

What are the implications, for politics and diplomacy, of Israeli fatigue, and of the intense self-absorption that is its corollary? What strikes one above all is how little attention Israelis are paying these days to their Arab neighbors. Sick of fighting, bent on building an Internet economy, they seem to have decided that Arabs feel the same way, and want the same things, they do. (In psychology, the term for this is projection.) According to a survey conducted by the Jaffee Center at Tel Aviv University, fully two-thirds of Israelis now agree with the following dubious assertions: that most Palestinians want peace; that signing agreements will end the Arab-Israeli conflict; and that if forced to choose between negotiations and increased military strength, Israel should opt for the former. Prime Minister Ehud Barak perfectly sums up this outlook in his repeated invocation of a peace that will "work for everyone," the unspoken assumption being that Arabs no less than Israelis seek to resolve their century-old conflict on harmonious terms.

Of course, at some level Israelis know full well about continued Arab rejectionism: the signs are too conspicuous for even the most ostrich-like to be truly clueless. But they have clearly chosen to de-emphasize or even ignore the phenomenon. How else to explain the absence of a single full-time Israeli journalist reporting from an Arab capital, or the fact that Hilal Khashan's meticulous survey of Arab opinion, with its thoroughly dismaying news, received no attention whatsoever in the Israeli press when it appeared last summer? "These are only words. Let them talk," is how Shimon Peres, speaking for many of his countrymen, has airily dismissed the undeniable evidence of Arab feelings and attitudes.

Peres's disdainful remark encapsulates a delusional but widespread Israeli assumption: that peace in the Middle East is Israel's for the making, and that if Israelis want to end the long-drawn-out struggle, they can do so on their own. They can "solve" the Palestinian problem by acceding to the creation of a state in the West Bank and Gaza; they can eliminate anti-Zionism by helping to funnel money to the Arabs, who will use their newfound affluence to become good neighbors (and never to amass more powerful arsenals); or—in the post-Zionist scenario—they can win Arab hearts by dismantling the Jewish attributes of the Jewish state.

Whatever the preferred tactic, the underlying premise is the same: that the key decisions of war and peace in the Arab-Israeli conflict are made in Jerusalem and Tel Aviv rather than—what is in fact the case— in Cairo, Gaza, Amman, and Damascus. Under the spell of this fantasy,

Israelis now seem prepared to execute what will amount to a unilateral transfer of hard-won territory—to Syria in the north, to the Palestinian Authority in the center of the country—in the hope that their troubles will thereby disappear. Indeed, they sometimes appear prepared to go to extreme lengths to induce their Arab interlocutors to accept the gifts they mean to confer on them.

Listening to the Israeli prime minister and the foreign minister of Syria as they inaugurated a new round of talks in December 1999, for example, one might have thought that Israel was the party that had instigated—and then lost—the Six-Day war of 1967, and was now desperately suing Damascus for terms. Barak spoke pleadingly of the need "to put behind us the horrors of war and to step forward toward peace," and of creating, "together with our Syrian partners, ... a different Middle East where nations are living side by side in peaceful relationship and in mutual respect and good-neighborliness." By contrast, the Syrian foreign minister blustered like a conqueror, insisting that Israel had "provoked" the 1967 clash and demanding the unconditional return of "all its occupied land." The very fact that a prime minister had agreed to meet with a mere foreign minister, breaching a cardinal protocol of diplomacy, was signal enough; that the foreign minister of Syria lacks any decision-making power whatsoever further confirmed who in this encounter was the wooer, who the wooed.

When it comes to Lebanon, Israelis appear to have convinced themselves that the unilateral withdrawal of troops from their "security zone" in the south will cause their main Lebanese opponent, Hezbollah, to leave them alone, despite repeated and overt statements by Hezbollah leadership that it intends to continue fighting until it reaches Jerusalem and that it "will never recognize the existence of a state called Israel even if all the Arabs do so." More, Israelis seem persuaded that the prospect of their withdrawal from Lebanon is one of the things that have the Syrians worried, quite as if the best way to scare your enemy were to threaten a retreat.

On the Palestinian track, the ostensibly more muscular party— Israel—has pointedly refrained from requiring that the ostensibly more vulnerable party fulfill the many obligations it has undertaken since 1993, with the result that the PA has neither turned over criminals and terrorists, nor ceased its unrelenting incitements to violence, nor restricted the size of its armed forces. The PA's logo brazenly shows a map of a future Palestine stretching from the Jordan River to the Mediterranean Sea—a Palestine, that is, not alongside Israel but instead of it. To all this, the Israeli body politic appears to pay no heed.

The newspaper *Ha'aretz* reports that Israeli negotiators have already conceded in principle to the Palestinian Authority the day-to-day control of parts of Jerusalem. At the very end of 1999, when Prime Minister Barak took the unprecedented step of releasing two Palestinian prisoners who had killed Israelis, his action was met, predictably, not with Arab gratitude but with noisy demonstrations chanting aggressive slogans—"Barak, you coward. Our prisoners will not be humiliated"—and by the demand that Israel now let go all of the estimated 1,650 jailed Palestinians. No doubt, the demonstrators will eventually get their way. Israelis are on their own road to peace, and no "partners," however hostile, will deflect them from it.

· · · · ·

Today's Israel, in sum, is hugely different from the Israel of old. For four decades and more, the country made steady progress vis-à-vis its enemies through the application of patience and will, backed when necessary by military courage and might. From a fledgling state in 1948 invaded by five Arab armies, it established itself as a powerful force, overcoming oil boycotts, terrorism, and the enmity of a superpower. But by the time of the Oslo accord of August 1993, the signs of exhaustion were becoming increasingly manifest; by now they are unmistakable.

As recently as the 1996 national elections, a lively debate took place in Israel over Palestinian noncompliance with the terms of Oslo and over the wisdom of handing the Golan Heights back to Syria. By the time of the 1999 elections, with very little having changed on the ground, those issues had disappeared. Perhaps 10 to 15 percent of the population still adheres to the old Likud view that Israel should keep control of the territories until the Arabs have shown a true change of heart. Today, the main debate is over timing and tone, not over substance. Symbolic of the new consensus is the fact that the Third Way, a party that was exclusively focused on retaining the Golan Heights under Israeli control and that took four Knesset seats in 1996, vaporized in 1999, winning not a single seat. Even former Prime Minister Benjamin Netanyahu, the reputed arch-hardliner, signed two empty agreements with Arafat and, on the Syrian track, was ready to concede virtually everything Hafez al-Assad demanded. As Ehud Barak has correctly noted, "there are only microscopic differences between the things Netanyahu was willing to discuss and those discussed by [Shimon] Peres and [Yitzhak] Rabin."

Many who bemoan the weakness of current Israeli policy are tempted to place the onus on Washington. But (to put it symbolically) how can one become exercised over Hillary Clinton's advocacy of a Palestinian state when, only weeks earlier, Shimon Peres had already specified a date for such a state's inception? Israelis are perfectly capable of choosing leaders prepared to resist American pressure, and they have done so in the past. The collapse of a meaningful opposition party in 1999—Menachem Begin won two elections as prime minister in 1977 and 1981, but last year his son and political heir had to withdraw from the race because his support was so trivial—rebuts the notion that weak politicians are doing the bidding of Washington; rather, they are doing the bidding of their electorate.

No, it is inward, to the Israeli spirit, that one must look for the roots of the present disposition to ignore repeated Palestinian flouting of solemnly signed agreements, to turn the Golan Heights over to a still-fanged Syria, to withdraw unilaterally from Lebanon, and to acquiesce in huge American sales of military equipment to an unfriendly and potentially threatening Egypt.

Israel today has money and weapons, the Arabs have will. Israelis want a resolution to conflict, Arabs want victory. Israel has high capabilities and low morale, the Arabs have low capabilities and high morale. Again and again, the record of world history shows, victory goes not to the side with greater firepower, but to the side with greater determination.

Among democracies, few precedents exist for the malaise now on display in Israel. Imperfect analogies include the atmosphere of pacifism and appeasement that pervaded significant sectors of opinion in France and England in the 1930s, the United States during the Vietnam period, and Western Europe in the early 1980s. But none of these situations quite matches Israel's in the extent of the debilitation. Even more critically, none of those countries lived with so narrow a margin of safety. France succumbed to the Nazis, but was able to recover. England nearly succumbed, but had time to rally with American help. The United States lost a long, bloody war in Vietnam, but the nation as a whole was hardly at risk. In Israel the stakes are far higher, the room for error correspondingly minute.

This is not to say that the Jewish state is in immediate danger; it continues to have a strong military and a relatively healthy body politic, and democracies have demonstrated the capacity to right their mistakes at five minutes to midnight. But one shudders to think of what calamity Israel must experience before its people wake up and assume, once again, the grim but inescapable task of facing the implacable enemies around them.

—*February 2000*

Norman Podhoretz

Intifada II:
Death of an Illusion?

"In my beginning is my end," wrote T. S. Eliot in words that are well suited to the Arab war against Israel. Although there is no end in sight to that war, the violence to which the Palestinians resorted in the wake of Ariel Sharon's visit to the Temple Mount on September 28 does at least mark the end of one act in this long and bloody drama. This was the act that began with the agreement at Oslo, which was then ratified on the White House lawn in September 1993 by Yasir Arafat, the chairman of the Palestine Liberation Organization (PLO), and Yitzhak Rabin, then the prime minister of Israel, with perhaps the most famous handshake in history.

So much diplomatic and political smoke has been blown in our eyes since that moment that a clear-sighted look at the act that opened then and is just now concluding requires us to step back and recapitulate. For even though we do indeed have here a near-perfect case of a beginning that was inexorably destined for the bitter end it has now reached, mighty efforts were made on all sides to persuade us that it would be otherwise.

In the early 18th century, the English theologian Bishop Joseph Butler said: "Things and actions are what they are, and the consequences of them will be what they will be: why then should we desire to be deceived?" About 200 years later, T. S. Eliot, to cite him again, gave us the answer to this breathtaking question when he observed in an entirely different context that "human kind/Cannot bear very much reality."

In this instance, the unbearable reality being evaded was that Israel's yearning for peace was shared neither by the Arab world in general nor by the Palestinians in particular—that their objection was not to anything Israel had done or failed to do, but to the very fact that it existed at all. Then, as time went on, and episode after episode occurred exposing the delusion of Oslo for what it was, more and more rationalizations had to be invented, and more and more lies had to be told, to keep it alive. Too much hope—and too much political capital—had been invested in the "peace process" to allow any opening of eyes that had been blinded and minds that had been closed by the dazzling mirage on the White House lawn.

No doubt believers in the idea that the road to peace had at last been found often directed these efforts to conceal the truth mainly at themselves. But they were hardly the sole or the exclusive objects of their own deceptions. On the contrary. The enthusiasm for Oslo—manifested, among many other ways, in the awarding of the Nobel Peace Prize to Yitzhak Rabin, his foreign minister Shimon Peres, and Yasir Arafat for having brought it about—was worldwide. So universal was it and so fervent that, with the ruthless unconcern of a tidal wave, it swept aside all doubts about the wisdom or the viability of the agreement.

Not, to be sure, in the Israeli public as a whole, where such doubts did continue to be harbored and, as we shall see, expressed from time to time in the electorate's choice of political leadership; but certainly in the major centers of opinion both in Israel and abroad, and wherever the writ of contemporary liberalism extended. In that vast domain, any Jew or for that matter any non-Jew (and there was a small brave band of them, an unhappy few) who voiced skepticism about Oslo immediately got stigmatized as an enemy of peace. This made him the moral equivalent, if not the de-facto ally, of Arab opponents of Oslo like the Muslim terrorists of Hamas and Hezbollah. Having been thus morally delegitimized, critics of the now-sacrosanct process were derided as well for their intellectual sins, accused of being too rigid to perceive that new developments had totally transformed the conflict between Israel and the Arab world.

· · · · ·

There were two distinct though complementary interpretations of these developments. One was the "realistic" analysis espoused by Rabin, the other a "visionary" picture painted by Peres.

As Rabin saw it, the demise of the Soviet Union had completely altered the old "strategic equation" in the Middle East by depriving the "frontline" Arab states of the armorer they had previously depended upon for engaging Israel militarily. In consequence, there was almost no likelihood that they would start any more conventional wars, as they had done several times in the past. This meant in effect that the Palestinians were now on their own; and while they could, on their own, assuredly make life miserable for Israel through terrorism, they were too weak to pose an "existential threat" to the Jewish state. The only serious such threat now came from the missiles of Iran and/or Iraq. To protect itself from that threat, Israel needed the help of the United States in building an effective system of antiballistic-missile defense.

In Rabin's view, then, the overriding strategic objective—merging military with political imperatives—was to ensure continued American support. How to do this? Well, the Americans were convinced (while not admitting it openly lest it arouse domestic political opposition) that giving the Palestinians a state of their own was the answer to unrest and instability throughout the Middle East. It followed that if Israel were to drop its "intransigent" resistance to this solution, relations with Washington would be more or less permanently shored up. This would in one stroke eliminate any future possibility that Israel might be denied the advanced military technology on which its survival now rested and that it could only get from the Pentagon.

My own guess is that Rabin in his heart of hearts was also motivated by the realization that Israel did not know how to deal effectively with the *intifada*, the new form of warfare that the Palestinians had now been waging for some six years. When the *intifada* first erupted in 1987, Rabin (then the defense minister under Yitzhak Shamir) had declared that he would "break the bones" of the Palestinian rioters. But breaking their bones did not avail, especially as the Palestinians—adopting a tactic that was at once brilliant and evil—were sending their *children* to throw stones at armed Israeli soldiers, most of all when TV cameras were present. In defending themselves and fighting back, even if only with rubber bullets, the Israelis inflicted casualties on these children, which inevitably tarnished their longstanding pride in their "purity of arms." In the end it was Rabin himself and a large segment of the Israeli people who were broken by the *intifada:* broken in spirit, broken in morale.

Prudently, Rabin never acknowledged anything like this in public. Nor did he ever make a speech explaining his overall strategy with respect to the United States. But it was no secret, having been spelled out in private to various friendly interlocutors. And others (in the course of trying to understand why Rabin was now crossing one "red line" after another that he had vowed never to cross) soon enough figured out what he had in mind. Of course, to understand the strategy did not necessarily entail agreeing with it. But disagreement, however carefully reasoned, had zero effect on Rabin and his battalions of cheerleaders.

Thus, it did no good whatsoever for critics of this analysis to observe that the United States was running into troubles of its own in constructing a defense against ballistic missiles. Admittedly, these troubles were more political than technological. Nevertheless, there was uncertainty as to whether the special aid from Washington on which Rabin was counting would ultimately be available.

Nor did it do the critics any good to pile up evidence that the State Department was flat-out wrong in its conviction that the Middle East would become more stable if a Palestinian state were to be established. As against the regnant cliché that the Palestinians were the "heart" of the region's problems, some of us pointed out that since Israel's birth in 1948 many wars had been fought among Arabs and/or Muslims over issues that had nothing to do with either the Jewish state or the Palestinians. Not only that, but the corpses produced by just one of these wars alone (Iran vs. Iraq) far exceeded the total number of casualties resulting from all those between the Arabs and Israel. Like every other argument we brought forth, this one too fell on deaf ears. Yet all by itself, it should have been enough to refute the dogma that "the key" to Middle Eastern stability was a Palestinian state under the despotic leadership of the PLO.

Moreover, there were many other grounds for expecting that a PLO state would breed more unrest and more instability than the present situation. To choose only the most obvious one, the fact that the majority of the population of Jordan was Palestinian could easily lead to a move by Arafat or his successors to take over that country, thereby creating the risk of an intervention by Syria (which had never ceased regarding not only Israel but also Lebanon and Jordan as "Southern Syria").

And none of this was even to mention the persistent refusal of the Palestinians themselves to surrender their claim on the entire territory lying within Israel's pre-1967 borders. (To this day, incredibly, despite at least three exultant announcements by Peres and Arafat that the articles of the Palestine National Covenant committing the PLO to the destruction of Israel had now definitely been repealed as mandated by Oslo, it remains unclear whether they actually ever were.) Nor did it touch upon the terrible problem that would arise with the million Palestinian citizens of Israel, some 800,000 of whom lived in the Galilee, where they constituted a majority. To which state would they remain loyal? Might they turn out to be a contemporary analogue of the German citizens of Czechoslovakia between the two world wars who became the pretext for Nazi Germany's phased conquest of that whole country?

· · · · ·

If there were deadly serious questions arising from the "realistic" analysis through which Rabin justified his embrace of Oslo, they were as nothing compared with the plain foolishness of Peres's vision of a "new Middle East." And if Rabin set foot on the path marked out by Oslo with misgivings and visible reluctance, Peres was so breathlessly eager that he fell all over himself in running toward it.

In the 1960's, a major slogan of the counterculture was "Make Love, Not War." Peres's vision of the new Middle East could be summarized in a variant of this catchy battlecry (and a battlecry, ironically, was what this pacifist slogan amounted to): "Make Money, Not War." Reading or listening to Peres, one might have imagined that a kind of vulgar-Marxist end of days had arrived in which the lion would not merely lie down with the lamb but go into business with it—both parties having discovered how much more pleasant it is to get rich than to fight, perchance to die.

To all appearances, the new faith Peres had adopted was not disturbed by the fact that, in the three or four years after Oslo, where the Arabs specifically pledged to renounce terrorism, about twice as many Israeli lives were lost to Palestinian suicide bombers than in the three or four years *before* the Arabs had presumably opted for money over war. Brushing off the grisly evidence of mangled corpses in the buses and marketplaces of Tel Aviv and Jerusalem—he and his supporters even took to characterizing the Jewish victims of these attacks as "martyrs to peace"—Peres went complacently on his visionary way. Though he never to my knowledge quoted Tertullian, the early father of the Church who declared of Christianity that he believed in it precisely because it was unbelievable, some such slogan could easily have become for Peres the spiritual complement, so to speak, of the materialistic "Make Money, Not War."

The complete fatuity of this notion was on vivid display at a 1994 conference in Morocco called by the Council on Foreign Relations (though I suspect the idea originally came from Peres). The purpose of the conference was to bring the nations of the Middle East together to formulate plans for cooperative economic development throughout the region. Here, if anywhere, was a chance for the Arab Middle East to signal that it had indeed arrived at a stage where it was more interested in making money by cooperating with Israel than in making war against it. Yet the delegation from Egypt—the first Arab country to have signed a peace treaty with Israel—showed up with a 90-page booklet containing a host of proposals in which the name of Israel was never once mentioned and illustrated by six maps of the Middle East on which the state of Israel did not appear. Meanwhile, in the military exercises of the Egyptian armed forces, Israel would continue to be cast as the presumptive enemy. So much for making money, not war.

Another component of Peres's vision of the "new Middle East," which dovetailed with Rabin's supposedly more hard-headed conception, was that the age of missiles had rendered territorial buffer zones obsolete. This assessment was intended to undermine the old conviction (once shared by all Israelis, emphatically including the younger Peres himself) that retreating to the boundaries in which Israel had lived before the Six-Day war of 1967, especially if a Palestinian state were left behind, was incompatible with the nation's security. But now, according to Peres, when land wars were becoming a thing of the past, so too was the notion of secure borders.

On this issue as well, abundant evidence to the contrary—most notably the Gulf war, which in the end had to be won (to the extent that it *was* won) by ground troops and tanks—was cavalierly ignored. Or else, like Palestinian terrorism, it was dismissed as just another hangover from a past that would soon be disposed of by History in its own species of mopping-up operation.

Yet while Peres himself may have kept the faith, stubbornly continuing to insist that he would not give terrorists a "victory" by abandoning the "peace process," the Israeli voting public disagreed. Running for prime minister in 1996 after the assassination of Rabin, Peres was beaten by Benjamin Netanyahu, who had been a strong critic of Oslo and would presumably adopt a tougher policy toward the Palestinians.

· · · · ·

In the event, Netanyahu disappointed many of his supporters by deciding to honor the Oslo agreement even though repeated Palestinian violations provided him with a legally sound case for backing out of it. True, while running for election, he had all but openly suggested that he *would* stick with Oslo. Yet if Rabin, in running for election some years earlier, had sworn never to negotiate with the PLO and then proceeded to do the opposite, why should Netanyahu have been expected to hold to his own campaign rhetoric?

But there was something even more disappointing to the hawks who had looked to Netanyahu for salvation from a "peace process" that they regarded as suicidal. This was the hesitant and inconsistent manner in which he enforced what he had most definitely promised: namely, to take no further steps along the Oslo road unless the Palestinians "reciprocated" by fully honoring their part of the bargain.

To the dismay of many who had assumed that *this* promise would at least be kept, Israeli territorial withdrawals went on under Netanyahu even though Arafat and his minions continued calling among themselves (but never when they spoke in Western languages to Western ears) for *jihad*, or "holy war," against Israel; even though Oslo was characterized (but, again, only in Arabic) as merely a stage in a multiphased struggle to wipe Israel off the map; and even though Palestinian schoolchildren were still being taught that Israel was an abomination that had to be eradicated. (Israeli schoolchildren, by contrast, were daily being offered history lessons that bent over backward to present the justice of the Palestinian claims.)

Palestinian violations of Oslo were by no means confined to the spoken word, or even to terrorism. For Arafat's Palestinian Authority (PA) was also stealthily building an army. Oslo had authorized a 24,000-man Palestinian police force armed only enough to maintain law and order within the territory Israel was ceding to the PA. Bizarre as it seems, the arms had been supplied by Rabin and Peres on the assumption that the PA police would relieve Israeli soldiers of the unpleasant necessity of policing these areas themselves. With a cynicism understandably bred by the double standard always being applied to Israel in these matters, Rabin once even remarked that whereas the Israelis were constantly being berated by human-rights organizations for trying to keep order, the Palestinians could be as brutal as they liked without running into much trouble from those same organizations. About this, he turned out to be largely right.

But so far as we can tell from the record, what Rabin never foresaw was that the Palestinians would not rest content with only 24,000 policemen, nor with the rifles they happily took from Israel. As the years passed, the number of "policemen" would rise to at least 40,000, and the heavier weapons precluded by Oslo would be smuggled in from Jordan and elsewhere. What Rabin also failed to anticipate—and did not live to see—was that the guns he had agreed to give the Palestinians would wind up being turned against Israelis, and that the police who were supposed to control rioters would instead join in with and even lead them.

. . . . .

The first time this happened was a kind of rehearsal for the violence we have just been living through. It occurred in September 1996, about three months after Netanyahu became prime minister, when a new exit was opened to an archeological tunnel in Jerusalem. Though work on this tunnel had been going on for years without objection from anyone, the new exit set off a Palestinian protest in Ramallah that soon spread through the West Bank and Gaza; and as it spread, it escalated. By the time Arafat had called a halt to the throwing of rocks and Molotov cocktails and the firing by Palestinian police on Israeli civilians and soldiers, who then fired back, 73 people were dead and some 1,500 injured.

Most of these were Palestinians, since in a firefight Israel still had a great advantage. To Arafat, however, this discrepancy in the number of casualties was more a source of pride than of regret. Had he not told the Palestinian police themselves only a week earlier that "our blood is cheap for Jerusalem"?

Besides, the whole incident could be and was exploited by Palestinian propaganda. According to the PA, the tunnel was intended by the Israelis to undermine the foundations of the al-Aqsa mosque on the Temple Mount, one of Islam's holiest places, and it was this nefarious enterprise that triggered the wholly justified rage of the Palestinians. Almost everyone in the world took the PA version of events at face value, and yet the most cursory glance at the situation would have shown that the allegation was blatantly false. As even the anti-Netanyahu editor of the *Biblical Archaeology Review* was constrained to acknowledge: "The tunnel is *outside* the Temple Mount. It threatens no religious sites. The al-Aqsa mosque is at the other end of the Temple Mount, as far away as you can get."

There were five lessons that should have hit home as a result of the tunnel episode. One was that the Palestinians felt no need to fulfill their main obligation under Oslo, which was to substitute negotiations for violence. This they more or less would do—if, that is, and only if, the negotiations were going their way. But if the Israelis did anything that displeased them, they would not hesitate to resort once again to force, even (or, with the media in mind, especially) if they themselves, and their children, were bound to suffer the heaviest casualties.

Was this enough to demonstrate that the critics of Oslo had been right all along in their belief that Israel did not have "a partner for peace" in Arafat? Not on your life. Rather than recognizing Arafat for what he was, and was not, much of the world decided that it was the Palestinians who did not have "a partner for peace" in Netanyahu. Having been denounced by his formerly most passionate supporters for refusing to abrogate Oslo, he now found himself vilified for sabotaging it. This charge was hurled at him by Jewish enthusiasts of Oslo within both Israel and America, as well as by the foreign ministries of virtually every country on earth, including the one in Washington, over which Bill Clinton, the allegedly "best friend" Israel had ever had, presided.

Yet all Netanyahu had done was to slow down the process a bit, and by means so trivial that after only a few years or even weeks no one could remember what they were. Even at the time, his political opponents and enemies had to go to almost comical lengths in drawing up an indictment against him. For example, in the words of one bill of particulars, his unforgivably major sins against the "peace process" consisted of (1) taking his time after being elected before deciding "to see Yasir Arafat"; (2) "making [Arafat] wait to travel in his helicopter within the West Bank"; and (3) "finally shaking hands with [Arafat] with a near grimace."

To this ridiculous list was added a number of more serious actions, but no hint was breathed that these same actions had also been taken by Peres when, in his brief tenure as prime minister after the assassination of Rabin, even he could not go on merely reaffirming his love of peace whenever another terrorist bomb exploded in Israel. (The main such actions by Peres were extending the deadline for a withdrawal from Hebron and sealing off the borders between Israel and the occupied territories.) Nor was there any mention of the things Netanyahu—eliciting even more furious disappointment among his old supporters—had done to mitigate or even reverse some of these policies he had inherited from Peres, like easing restrictions on the number of Arab workers allowed into Israel from the territories every day, and going through with the pullout from Hebron.

A second lesson of the tunnel episode, then, was that the term "peace process" was itself a fraud. It did not mean what the words normally signified: negotiations aiming at a yet-to-be-hammered-out agreement between parties previously at war. Rather, it was a deceptive euphemism for steady Israeli movement toward a predetermined end, which was the turnover of the West Bank and Gaza to a new Palestinian state. Any slowing of the pace for any reason was condemned as "foot-dragging," and even the slightest indication from the Israeli side that the Palestinians would not get everything they wanted was interpreted

as contrary to the spirit of the peace process and a provocation that justified them in once again picking up the gun.

· · · · ·

Which brings us to the third lesson yielded by the tunnel episode. Among
the great achievements to which enthusiasts of Oslo and its aftermath
proudly pointed was that Israel was becoming increasingly less isolated.
Before Oslo, cooed the doves, Israel's only friend of any consequence had
been the United States; and within the Arab world, only Egypt had been
willing to make peace with the Jewish state, and only a "cold peace" at
that. Now, however, Israel was ceasing to be a pariah. Even at the United
Nations, which had for so long been viciously hostile, the atmosphere
had grown warmer; and, more telling still, commercial and other relations were being established with some of the more moderate Arab states.

All true; but what the tunnel episode revealed was that every bit
of this good will would vanish the instant Israel made a single false
move—that is, a move that the Palestinians declared to be false. At the
UN, a Security Council resolution condemning Israel over the tunnel
incident passed by a vote of 14-0, with the United States under Bill Clinton—in a preview of what he would do in October of this year—abstain-
ing when it might have exercised its veto.

As for the Arab world, even the states that had traditionally been
least hostile to Israel now ganged up on it. The dovish *Jerusalem Report*
summed up the situation:

> King Hassan of Morocco ... ordered a complete freeze on his gov-
> ernment's relations with Israel.... The president of Tunis ... fol-
> lowed suit and ordered formal contacts between his country and
> the Netanyahu government severed. Oil-rich Qatar ... postponed
> the opening of [its] trade office in Israel and called off direct meet-
> ings with Israeli officials.

This report was supposed to prove that Netanyahu had done great damage to Israel. But what it inadvertently exposed was that any warming
trend among the Arabs would turn to solid ice the moment they suspected
that Israel might be stalling in its journey toward the only acceptable conclusion of the "peace process": complete withdrawal (with minor modifications) to the borders of 1967 and the recognition of a Palestinian state
in the territories Israel had conquered in the Six-Day war of that year.

Even this, however, would not suffice—and here we arrive at the
fourth lesson of the tunnel episode. In a moment of candor, Arafat him-

self admitted that he had started the miniwar over the tunnel to fight against "the Judaization of Jerusalem." The only acceptable "peace package," in other words, had to be stuffed with the gift of East Jerusalem as the capital of the new Palestinian state. No Jerusalem, no deal.

To this a codicil was added, and it represents the fifth and final lesson to emerge from the tunnel episode. If Israel would not deliver the right "peace package," the alternative was another war—a war not between Israel and the Palestinians alone but between Israel and the whole Arab world. Even Egypt, which had signed a peace treaty with Israel years earlier, and Jordan, which had just done the same, would participate in this war.

That a major war was in the minds of the Arab leaders became—or should have become—obvious during one of those hastily arranged meetings that Bill Clinton loves to call whenever another crisis erupts between Israel and the Palestinians. (Arafat, astoundingly, holds the record for the number of visits with Clinton by foreign leaders.) At the meeting to resolve the tunnel crisis, the late King Hussein of Jordan, that famous moderate, excoriated Netanyahu for having dragged the region to "the edge of the abyss." In spelling out his meaning a few days later, he had the impudence to bring up the Iraqi missile attacks on Israel during the Gulf war, when he himself had sided with Saddam Hussein to the point of providing targeting guidance to Iraqi controllers as their missiles—with the blessing of the "little king"—flew over Jordanian air space.

Having been forgiven, as he always was no matter what he did, thus spake King Hussein: "In the current situation, if we do not stride strongly forward to achieve peace, everything imaginable can happen, including a revival of 1991 when Netanyahu wore his gas mask on television. The alternative to peace is more awful than we can imagine."

And what of that other famous moderate, the Egyptian president Hosni Mubarak? Since he had recently described Israel as "a knife plunged into the nations of this region"—note the words "nations of this region" rather than "Palestinians"—it is not surprising that Mubarak should have refused to attend the White House meeting at all. Coupled with this refusal was a warning that the Palestinians would soon take up arms again, and through his former military chief of staff Mubarak also warned that Egypt and the other Arab states would be ready to rush into the battle with every expectation of victory: "The combined weaponry of the Arab states today exceeds that of Israel. If all these weapons were directed against Israel, the Arab states could defeat Israel."

Then we come to Hafez al-Assad, the late president of Syria. No one ever confused him with a moderate, but in spite of the "strategic decision for peace" he had supposedly made, Assad decided a few weeks after the White House summit that Israel was—in the words of one of his spokesmen—"preparing the region for a new war," and that the Arabs now had "to consider options other than the peace process." Note again that the war for which preparations had to be made was not between Israel and the Palestinians alone, but between Israel and the *Arabs*.

· · · · ·

When Ehud Barak of the Labor party, defeating the by-now much-battered Netanyahu, became prime minister of Israel in 1999, he was widely hailed as a disciple of Rabin who would put his martyred predecessor's policies back on track. And so he did—with a veritable vengeance. No one could accuse *him* of "dragging his feet" or of insisting on "reciprocity," and the only defect he could find in the Oslo "peace process" was that it was being implemented too slowly. In this he seemed to resemble Peres more than Rabin, raring to go, chafing at the bit, hardly able to wait before satisfying all Palestinian demands as quickly as possible—and to make a deal with Syria while he was at it. To judge both from Barak's statements and his behavior, the tunnel war might never have happened, so apparently oblivious was he of the lessons it had taught about the realities of Israel's situation and the intentions of the Arab world.

Accordingly, Barak cut immediately to the chase. Among the first things he did was to pledge an early withdrawal of Israeli troops from the security zone in Lebanon that, with the aid of local militiamen, they had been policing since 1982 in order to protect northern Israel from terrorist and other attacks by the Hezbollah—a pledge that he subsequently carried out under fire and ahead of his one-year schedule. Barak also indicated that he was willing to return virtually the whole of the Golan Heights to Syria in exchange for a peace treaty. And he declared himself ready to skip the type of interim steps and phased agreements with the Palestinians that were the progeny of Oslo. What he preferred was to discuss the terms of a final settlement. Which meant that precisely the *most* difficult problems—the status of Jerusalem, and what should be done about the Palestinians who had fled in 1948 and so many of whose descendants were still living in squalid refugee camps throughout the region—would be tackled now, and not (as formerly contemplated) be deferred to some later date when greater trust would presumably have developed between the parties.

So far did Barak's proposals go that in time they would even arouse the ire of Rabin's widow, Leah, who had previously anointed the new prime minister as her late husband's legitimate heir. But what had once been unthinkable, and unsayable even by Rabin and Peres, was by now so taken for granted that it practically went without saying at all: a sovereign Palestinian state would soon be established. The only remaining question was whether this would be delayed until its exact boundaries, the location of its capital, and a few other matters had been determined by negotiations with Israel, or whether Arafat would make good on his repeated threat to bring it into being unilaterally.

While letting slip one deadline after another for acting on this threat, Arafat found himself on the receiving end of offers that went beyond anything ever contemplated by any previous Israeli government. Although one would never have known this from the tenor of most reporting in the media, and certainly not from Palestinian propaganda about the onerous Israeli "occupation," 98 percent of the Palestinians in the territories were already living under the rule of the PA. With the Israeli army having withdrawn from most of those territories before he assumed office, Barak now proposed to turn over virtually all the rest to the new Palestinian state (with Israel left holding, on grounds of military security, only a small and largely unpopulated area). Barak even offered to leave the Jordan Valley, which had once been regarded by all sides in Israel as essential to the country's security.

Nor was this all. Barak—again conceding what had recently been unthinkable—would accept certain districts in East Jerusalem as the capital of the new state of Palestine, while turning over the holy places to international supervision. Finally, and in some ways most radically of all, he was willing to grant the "right of return" to some 100,000 Palestinian refugees and compensate the remainder with money that Clinton (a little too confidently) assured him would be forthcoming from America.

All this might have been too much even for Rabin's widow, but it was not enough for Yasir Arafat. He demanded a larger share of Jerusalem and complete control over the Temple Mount, the site of the al-Aqsa mosque and the Dome of the Rock (the latter repeatedly and mistakenly described in the media as a mosque). Under no circumstances would he entertain Barak's suggestion that a small sector of the Temple Mount be reserved for a synagogue. The Temple Mount belonged to Allah, and what Barak wanted was nothing less than a desecration and a blasphemy.

And so the stage was set for a replay of the tunnel war, one that would be bigger and more portentous than its predecessor. But before we can grasp what really happened, we must again clear the smoke away from several points that have—in the usual fashion of reporting on clashes between Israel and the Palestinians—been obscured either through ignorance or deliberate misrepresentation.

· · · · ·

For a start, take the issue of the Temple Mount itself. Because there is a place called Mount Zion in Jerusalem, many people are under the impression that *it* is the site from which—as Jews (quoting the prophet Isaiah) proclaim whenever they remove the Torah scroll from the ark of a synagogue—the law and the word of God will go forth unto the nations. But the Zion of this prophecy-turned-prayer is not Mount Zion. It is the Temple Mount, so named precisely because King Solomon built his Temple there in the 10th century B.C.E.; and when, about a century after the destruction of that Temple by Babylonian invaders in 586 B.C.E., a second one was built, it too was located on the same site until being destroyed by the Romans in 70 C.E.* And as if this were not enough, Jewish tradition also identifies the Temple Mount as the Mount Moriah of the Bible where God tested Abraham by commanding him to sacrifice his son Isaac and then stayed his hand.

In other words, the Temple Mount is the holiest of Jewish holy places, and has been so for at least 3,000 years—which means that the Jewish claim on it goes back over 1,500 years before there even was an Islam. Furthermore, whereas Jerusalem has been the center of Judaism since King David made his capital there in the 10th century B.C.E., the city is, by the Muslims' own reckoning, only the third holiest place in their religion. When Muslims pray, they do not face Jerusalem, as Jews do; they face Mecca.

In short, there is nothing in the least outrageous about the idea that the Temple Mount belongs to the Jews, though it was not even accessible to them during the years before 1967 when the Jordanians occupied Jerusalem. But in his notorious visit on September 28, Sharon was not even demanding that Israel physically take over the Temple Mount (which under Israeli sovereignty had long been administered by the Muslim authorities); all he was doing, as leader of the Likud opposition, was putting Barak *and* Arafat on notice that he would work against any agreement curtailing the right of any Jew to visit the Temple Mount whenever he wished.

---

*The Western Wall is a section of the retaining wall of the Second Temple. Though never part of the Temple Mount as such, it has nevertheless been sanctified by proximity as well as by the protective function it once served.

It is Arafat who has made it necessary to emphasize what ought to be a self-evident point. For just as much of the Arab world has joined the chorus of Holocaust deniers in the West, so with comparable gall does Arafat go around declaring that "Jerusalem is not a Jewish city, despite the biblical myth planted in some minds"; that the two Temples never stood on the Temple Mount; and that the Western Wall is not a Jewish but "a Muslim shrine."

Some think that in going to the Temple Mount, Sharon was also trying to upstage his main rival for leadership of Likud, the politically resurgent Netanyahu. But even if that is true, what difference would it make to the assignment of blame for the outbreak of violence by the Palestinians in response to a peaceful walk around the site—a walk, we have since learned, that a day earlier had been duly cleared with the head of PA security? In retrospect, considering how unlikely it is that the head of PA security was ignorant of the plan for an outbreak, and in the light of reports that he himself had a hand in fomenting the riots, one wonders whether he was setting Sharon up by assuring him that there would be no problem if he were to visit the Temple Mount.

· · · · ·

Be that as it may, we have also since learned that preparations for violence were already being made immediately before and during the summit between Arafat and Barak that Clinton had convened in July at Camp David. If, said a high-ranking PA security official quoted in an Israeli Arab magazine, the summit were to fail from the Palestinian point of view, a new *intifada* would follow:

> The Palestinian people are in a state of emergency against the failure of the Camp David summit. If the situation explodes they are ready for the next bloody battle against the Israeli occupation. The next *intifada* will be ... more violent than the first one especially since the Palestinian people [now] possess weapons allowing them to defend themselves in a confrontation with the Israeli army.†

---

†For this and most of the other quotations that follow from Arabic-language sources, I am indebted to the invaluable work of the Middle East Media Research Institute (MEMRI). Under the leadership of Yigal Carmon, a former adviser on counterterrorism to both Yitzhak Shamir and Yitzhak Rabin, MEMRI monitors the Palestinian media, as well as the press of other Arab nations, and issues daily translations into English of significant articles and interviews that are rarely, if ever, noticed in Western coverage of the Middle East. MEMRI's website is at www.memri.org.

Regarding those weapons, this PA official then went on a week later (that is, *two full months* before Sharon would set foot on the Temple Mount) to inform the same magazine that

> Popular recruitment in the PA territories has increased greatly and the popular Palestinian army has been established.... Weapons have already been distributed to citizens by the PA, which supervises training and preparation for a potential confrontation with occupation forces.

Finally, the commander of the PA police stated that "the Palestinian police will be leading, together with all other noble sons of the Palestinian people, when the hour of confrontation arrives."

When the summit did in fact fail, and when Clinton was perceived as blaming Arafat for turning down Barak's terms, which seemed even to the President extraordinarily generous, rocks and Molotov cocktails were at the ready, and the militiamen (or Tanzim) of Fatah, Arafat's own faction within the PLO, were lying in wait for an order from him to go on a rampage. In seizing on Sharon's visit as the right moment for such a signal, Arafat must have calculated that even though, as the leader of the Likud party, Sharon held no office within the Labor government, as a right-winger he was likely to be held responsible for the violence, exactly in the way the right-wing Netanyahu had been for the miniwar over the tunnel. And so it came about.

Despite the assurances of the PA security chief, violent disturbances broke out just moments after Sharon left the area. The Palestinian media and Muslim preachers immediately began spreading the word that al-Aqsa was in danger. The next day, September 29, in a sermon at the mosque itself, the mullah accused Sharon of the "slighting of Muslims' holy place," and asked: "Who will forbid the Jews from committing massacres today in al-Aqsa mosque?" The same kind of false, hysterical, and inflammatory rhetoric concerning al-Aqsa had been spewed forth over the tunnel, and it worked even more effectively in this latest battle against "the Judaization of Jerusalem."

So, too, did the tactic of taking casualties for the TV cameras to photograph. Echoing Arafat's statement of 1996 that "our blood is cheap for Jerusalem," the director general of the PA information ministry now wrote: "The only way to impose our conditions is inevitably through our blood. Had it not been for this blood, the world would never have been interested in us." Hence it was the "national duty" of the Palestinians to "continue to sacrifice our martyrs."

Palestinian and other Arabs had a lot of takers both in Israel and in the rest of the world for their assertion that it was Sharon who had provoked this latest outbreak of violence. But Barak was not among them. Partly, no doubt, because he had come to believe that his own political fortunes would be improved if he could persuade a reluctant Sharon to join him in a national-unity government, but also, surely, because he knew what he knew, Barak disagreed with the widespread condemnation of the visit to the Temple Mount. "We hold the Palestinian Authority responsible for the whole round of violence," he told Lally Weymouth in an interview in *Newsweek*.

·　·　·　·　·

What then lies ahead? As noted at the outset, it was to some degree because the situation that obtained prior to 1993 had involved Israel in the kind of guerrilla-cum-terrorist warfare it finally could not stomach that Rabin decided to enter into the "peace process" to begin with. Now, there has been a resurgence of precisely that kind of warfare. Will the Israelis be any more able and willing to stomach it this time around?

In trying to answer that question, we have to consider two opposing factors. One is that the Palestinians, as they have boasted, are far better armed than they were before and capable of inflicting more damage than they could in the first round. But as against that consideration, there is the balancing emergence of a new mood in Israel. By making as many concessions as they did—walking, as it were, the extra mile toward peace—and then being rewarded with violence, most Israelis, beginning with Prime Minister Barak himself, seemed to have been convinced for the moment that there was no corresponding desire for peace on the Palestinian side. If so, the delusory hopes that pushed them into the "peace process" and fed it for nearly a decade might give way to a greater readiness to face the grim realities of their own situation.

To illustrate, two examples should suffice. Shlomo Avineri, a professor at the Hebrew University and a former director-general of the foreign ministry, was among the earliest and most influential Israeli proponents of the two-state solution. But he now wrote in the *Jerusalem Post* that, in having persuaded themselves that a compromise with the Palestinians had become possible, he and his fellow doves were caught up in an "illusion":

> Last summer at Camp David, Arafat rejected the most generous offer ever made to a Palestinian leader by an Israeli statesman.... [Then] it suddenly dawned on us that we do not have a partner: only an enemy, who cannot even find a humane word when our people are lynched.... What came out—on the streets, among the

Palestinian elite on CNN—was sheer hatred, and a fundamental rejection of Israel.... [So] now we know: there is no such thing as a Palestinian leadership with whom an agreement can be reached. We are at war.

On a different level of the Israeli social spectrum, there was the mother of three in Jerusalem who was interviewed by the Associated Press. Like Avineri, she had been a supporter of the "peace process" from the start, but this woman (also like Avineri, and like almost all Israelis) was shaken to her toes by the murder and mutilation of two Israeli reservists who had mistakenly driven into Ramallah: "When I saw on television the Palestinian mob that lynched those two Israeli soldiers, I realized they don't want peace with us. There was such hatred in their eyes. They just want us out of the Middle East."

They just want us out of the Middle East. This is a fundamental truth that all Israelis once knew but that many either forgot or began to deny. Now they seemed to be remembering and relearning it; and in the nick of time. For they will need every ounce of spiritual and moral strength at their disposal to cope with the reality to which so many of them blinded themselves for so long.

That reality, to say it yet one more time, is summed up in the word— *jihad*—that Arafat and so many other Arabs have never stopped invoking when speaking among themselves in their own language. On those occasions, they have never bothered to pretend that the formula for peace is a "two-state solution." Nor have they had to pretend that this formula represents anything more than a temporary abandonment of the direct military action that failed in five previous wars, or a shift to a "strategy of stages" that will more circuitously and cunningly head toward the same ultimate consummation in the destruction of the Jewish state. Indeed, at this very moment, Palestinian and other Arab children are studying textbooks containing maps on which (as in the Egyptian proposals for regional economic development at the conference in Morocco) Israel is nowhere to be found. It is the making of such maps into a real picture of the Middle East that—to judge by their own words and deeds— remains the true objective of overwhelming numbers of Palestinians and their Arab brothers. Listen to a leading Egyptian cleric—and bear in mind that to him "occupied Palestine" embraces the whole state of Israel:

Jihad in the path of Allah is a virtue that binds Muslims at all times, and it is an obligation on everyone who is able to carry it out....

Jihad to confront the enemy and liberate the pillaged land is an obligation on Muslims.... This is what our brothers are now doing in occupied Palestine.

When evidence was presented at his trial in Jerusalem that Adolf Eichmann, the former Nazi officer in charge of transporting the Jews of Europe to the death camps, had once said he would "die happy" because he had sent five million "enemies of the Reich" (i.e., Jews) to their graves, Hannah Arendt dismissed this as "sheer rodomontade." Is the exhortation to *jihad* by so many Arabs, from Arafat to the likes of this Egyptian cleric, sheer rodomontade? There is no more reason to think so than there was in the case of Eichmann.

A few years ago, Fouad Ajami of Johns Hopkins produced what may still be the best short article ever published on sentiment toward Israel within the Arab world—and perhaps the only such honest account by any Arab anywhere. "There has been no discernible change in the Arab attitudes toward Israel," he maintained in *U.S. News & World Report,* and went on to describe the genuine state of affairs in the world from which he himself (a Lebanese Christian by birth and upbringing) had come to the United States:

> The great refusal [to accept Israel] persists. A foul wind ... blows in that "Arab street" of ordinary men and women, among the intellectuals and the writers, and in the professional syndicates. The force of this refusal can be seen in the press of the governments and of the oppositionists, among the secularists and the Islamists alike, in countries that have concluded diplomatic agreements with Israel and those that haven't.

Only a few weeks ago, with the new *intifada* raging, Ajami observed that his original assessment still held:

> The circle of enmity surrounding Israel has not been breached—the young boys in the West Bank displayed their great refusal to come to terms with Israel's statehood; so did the demonstrators in Arab lands, from North Africa to the Persian Gulf, whose rulers had staked a claim to moderation. Diplomacy was shown to be a pretense and a veneer.

Some of us even thought for a while that this new *intifada* might be the start of the big war—the war with missiles and tanks and heavy artillery rather than rocks and gasoline bombs and rifles—we had always feared would result from the "peace process." Arafat and his subordinates seem to have thought so, too. "Palestinian blood [will] mix with Arab blood in defense of the legitimate rights of our people," Arafat announced on October 8 in Tunis. Another PA official was more specific:

> The continuation of the Palestinian bloodshed might push part of the Arab military to carry out military operations against Israel.... Also, Palestinian bloodshed will push parts of the Arab countries to launch missiles against Israel as the president of Iraq did in 1991.

Then, the very next day, Saddam Hussein himself actually threatened to take the lead in "putting an end to Zionism," or even to go it alone if the other Arab states held back.

Fortunately for Israel, and the world, most of the Arab states were not yet ready to engage Israel militarily. In late October, sixteen of the 22 member states of the Arab League met in Cairo to decide on what they should do about the current crisis. But while blasting Israel for its "crimes" and resolving to cut off relations of various kinds with it, they stopped so far short of declaring "holy war" that the Libyan delegates walked out in disgust at this "feeble" response, and the Iraqis were if anything even more contemptuous.

Meanwhile, demonstrations were being held all over the Arab world, demanding *jihad* and denouncing the Arab governments for being "too soft on Israel." For the time being, then, what Ajami calls "the peace of kings and pharaohs" still prevails. But how long can it withstand the pressures for war from every sector of Arab society?

· · · · ·

As long, I would say, as the kings and pharaohs of the contemporary Middle East are deterred by the fear of Israel's armed might and the willingness of Israel to use it if necessary. About seven years ago, when the "peace process" was just getting under way, I gave a lecture in Jerusalem predicting that this process would lead not to peace but to another major war. During the question period, a leading dove amazed the audience by expressing total agreement with me. But, he added, "unless we convince our sons that we are doing everything possible to make peace, they will jump out of their tanks when the war comes."

He may have been right. From which one might conclude that the "peace process" was an exercise that had to be undergone if only to expose the main illusions behind it. Those illusions went beyond the idea that a compromise with the Palestinians had become possible. They extended to the notion that Israel bore at least as much blame for the Arab war against it as the Arabs did; that, if Israel were to reconcile itself to the establishment of a Palestinian state, the Arab world would reconcile itself to a Jewish one; and that it was in Israel's unilateral power to realize this vision of peaceful coexistence.

But the dream of wiping Israel off the map was not put into Arab heads by anything Israel did except enter into existence, and therefore it could not be canceled by anything Israel did except disappear. Neither the Palestinians nor their Arab brothers would remain satisfied with a Palestinian state living alongside Israel; what they wanted was a Palestinian state that would swallow up the Jewish state. And the only peace that could be achieved through the unilateral power of Israel was the peace of the grave that committing suicide would bring.

If they are finally learning all this, the sons of the older Israelis who had to relearn it themselves will not "jump out of their tanks" when the next major war erupts. But that alone could help avert such a war, by deterring the Arabs who had begun to believe, and not without good cause, that Israel was growing soft and would soon be ripe for the plucking. A strong Israel—strong not only in weaponry but in resolve and courage and the readiness to do whatever might be necessary to prevent the worst— could fend off the *jihad* that might otherwise be all but inevitable.

It could also fend off what the Israeli defense analyst Ze'ev Schiff thinks is the strategy for "bringing Israel to its knees" that Arafat has hit upon as a fallback or a prelude to *jihad*. This, according to Schiff, is "ongoing, low-level war that combines massive terrorism, guerrilla warfare, and the international media.... This strategy will expose Israel's Achilles' heel: an extreme sensitivity to loss of life and the kidnapping of its soldiers."

No corresponding sensitivity undermines the Palestinians. In an exceptionally objective piece, Jack Kelley of *USA Today,* describing a firefight in Ramallah in October, reported that "As darkness moves in, many of the television journalists, who had been filming on the Palestinian side ... pack up their gear and leave. So do the youths." Kelley then, with no hint of a personal demurrer, quoted an Israeli officer on the spot: "The kids only want to die when the TV cameras are on so they can get the sympathy of the world. They'll be back tomorrow, as soon as the media arrive."

But why, asked Mark Helprin in his column in the online *Opinion Journal* of the *Wall Street Journal,* do not the Israelis—understanding full well that every youthful Palestinian casualty hurts them and strengthens Arafat in "the battle of public opinion"—use less lethal methods of riot control? To his own question, Helprin returned this answer:

> Because they cannot.... Every day, from the periphery and from within the rock-throwing and gasoline-bomb-tossing crowds,

automatic fire is directed at the Israelis, who are thus forced to use small-unit tactics and keep themselves dispersed. The Israelis cannot close with the crowds, using shields and batons, because to do so they would need to concentrate hundreds or perhaps thousands of men in these battles, soldiers who in such antiquated formations would be a vulnerable and irresistible target.

In sum, up to that point in the new *intifada*, the Israelis were doing what they had to do. Palestinian propagandists were having a field day proclaiming that the Israelis were "massacring . . . innocent children." But the complaint of many Israelis was that the army had been showing too much restraint on occasions like the gunfire attacks on a Jewish neighborhood within Jerusalem itself. On the other hand, as the officer whom Kelley accompanied during the battle that day said to him, with regret but without apology, and without the sense of guilt that had turned round one of the *intifada* into a victory for the Palestinians: "Since the first day, every time we shoot a person, it is because they . . . shot at us first. You don't want to shoot civilians and kids. On the other hand, you don't want your soldiers on the frontlines to be killed."

· · · · ·

Writing in late October 2000, I have no idea of what either Barak or Arafat will do in the next few weeks, or what might be triggered by this or that step one or the other might take. One such step by the Israelis might be toward "separation," about which the new *intifada* unleashed so much talk in Israel.

Why, it was said, could Israel not unilaterally draw its own borders and leave Arafat to his own devices on the other side, relying on deterrence to protect the country from terrorist or other forms of aggression? This, for Israel, would be a substitute for a negotiated settlement, still acceding to the birth of a Palestinian state though backing away from Barak's former willingness to recognize neighborhoods in East Jerusalem as its capital. (Amid all this talk about unilateral moves by Israel, Barak also warned the Palestinians that if *they* were to issue a unilateral declaration of statehood, he would annex parts of the West Bank. To which Arafat countered with a threat of an even wider state of war.)

Even at this early date, however, it can safely be predicted that no unilateral actions by Israel such as are simplistically contemplated by the repentant Shlomo Avineri and others would bring about what most Israelis envisage as "separation." As Ephraim Sneh, Israel's deputy minister of defense, commented to the *New York Times:* "People say, 'I don't want to see anymore the Palestinians,' ... but it doesn't work that way. The interdependence of the economies is such that you can't just detach them mechanically. We share water, electricity, electromagnetic space. It's not so simple."

Shlomo Gazit, a former general and government official, also quoted by the *Times,* brought up other difficulties attendant upon a real separation: "It means annexing the West Bank with its settlers, but also evacuating others." Gazit could not bring himself to state clearly, or possibly even to contemplate, that "evacuating others" might involve not only Palestinians in the West Bank but also Arab citizens of Israel, together with non-Israeli Palestinians who live in East Jerusalem. It is hard to imagine the Israelis undertaking so brutal an act of "ethnic cleansing," and still harder to suppose that the West would allow them to carry it through even if they made the attempt.

The upshot is that under present circumstances, there are no good alternatives, only choices that may be less bad than others. Still, present circumstances will not last forever. History could yet hit the Middle East with one of those unexpected surprises in which it specializes (such as the sudden collapse of the Soviet Union) and that would for the first time create a willingness among the Arabs to make their own inner peace with the permanent presence of a sovereign Jewish state in "their" part of the world. But unless and until such a change of heart cancels out "the great refusal," the change of heart in Israel that the new *intifada* seemed to have wrought in certain quarters will have to remain firm against the seductive temptations of a return to some new form of Oslo. It will also have to remain firm against the loudly intransigent insistence in other quarters that the "peace process" can and must be revived.

It is from those other quarters that the "post-Zionist" virus of self-hatred has spread in recent years, sapping the national morale and the old-time national resolve. To regain what they have lost, the Israelis will have to shake off this pathology once and for all; they will have to rely credibly once again on the deterrent effect of their military might; they will have to renew their conviction that their country has an absolute right to exist where it exists; and they will have to recapture the well-earned and well-deserved pride they used to feel in the miracle of that existence and the wondrous accomplishments that have followed from the Jewish return to Zion.

—December 2000

Fiamma Nirenstein

The Journalists and the Palestinians

The information coming out of Israel these days is heavily influenced by the political imagination of the reporters and columnists and cameramen who have flocked to the scene from the four corners of the earth to cover this latest installment of violence in the ongoing Middle East conflict. They tend—they are *expected*—to place those clashes within an agreed-upon framework: the framework, roughly, of David (the Palestinians) versus Goliath (the Israelis). It is only when they fail to follow this paradigm that they, their editors, and their readers or viewers become confused.

And no wonder. Imagine a weary journalist, getting back to his office or press room in Jerusalem at the end of a hard day: how is he to begin describing what he has seen? The events he must try to present are, in truth, terribly complicated, and, when it comes to an informed perspective, he himself is often wet behind the ears. As for the subtle interplay between what in the swirl of events is cause and what is effect, between the norms of Western and Eastern civilizations, between democracy and dictatorship, between the Judeo-Christian world and the world of Islam—all this gets lost in the confusion of daily armed clashes and terror bombings, so alien to the normal rhythms of normal societies.

And so, like the morning mists that envelop the city of Jerusalem, the reality of the situation often dissipates into a fog made up of the psychological impulses and fixed ideas of those observing it. From an elevated spot like the suburb of Gilo, where I happen to live, the local geography does in fact sometimes disappear in the mist, and Jerusalem itself can seem transformed into a white lake. My neighbors and I are left only with the explosions of firearms aimed in our direction from the nearby Arab village of Beit Jalla, and the furious responses of Israel's Apache helicopters.

And what about the view from East Jerusalem? In the Arab city, from early morning on, the international media breathe the perfumed mist of something indescribably romantic and archaic mingled with the aroma of youthful furor. In the fog, the Jerusalem of the Jews must loom in the imagination like a powerful machine, an established mass pushing with its force and its money on a weaker, newborn world. The fog offers an opportunity, a screen, against which foreign correspondents project the attitudes they came with: their reflexive critiques of capitalism, of consumerism, of globalization, even of themselves and their own societies.

The American Colony, a lovely old hotel in East Jerusalem, is home to almost all the international journalists who have come here on temporary assignment. The ancient vine-covered stone is part of the hotel's charm, and so too is its storied past, redolent of travelers' tales, of miraculous reunions after shipwrecks at sea and near-escapes in faraway climes. Above all, its charm derives from the discreetness and quiet of the remote little street where it stands, a symbol of understatement amid the vertiginous passions of the surrounding environs.

Not far away runs Salah-al-Din, the central thoroughfare of Arab Jerusalem, all stores, noises, traffic jams. Here is where some of the Friday clashes take place, after morning prayers at the mosques. By evening, the restaurant at the American Colony has become packed with dusty, tired journalists, just back with their cell phones and notebooks from Gaza or Ramallah, from the areas of shooting. They are, most of them, between the ages of thirty-five and fifty, old enough to appreciate a moment of relaxation. In this comradely setting one feels the extraordinary informal power of the media—iconoclastic, sporty, ironic, virtually all of one mind.

The support crews are largely Arab, the stringers Palestinian and often the cameramen, too. The hotel waiters and staff are likewise Palestinian, as are the regular guests one runs into in the halls, left over from the time of the *intifada* of the late 1980's—the first *intifada*, the real one. The leaders of that uprising regard the American Colony as their private stomping ground, a place for keeping appointments, for conducting interviews, for jocularly confiding in foreign newsmen. An acquaintance amusedly tells me of overhearing a correspondent thanking his Palestinian source for supplying him with the precise hours of the next day's "spontaneous" clashes.

. . . . .

The American Colony—with its reassuring air of Arab refinement, the plashing of the fountain in the hotel's paradisiacal little garden where breakfast is served amid jasmine and roses, its white and blue Armenian tiles, its Eastern touches adjusted to Western tastes, the friendliness of its staff cloaked in courtesy and dignity—is much more than a hostelry: it is a metaphor for the sympathy the international press harbors for the Palestinian cause and, conversely, its complex animosity toward Israel. Slightly vain, many of the guests here still bask in memories of themselves at age twenty, Arab *kaffias* around their necks, on the campuses of American or European universities: young rebels, young heroes, young upsetters of the hegemonic powers-that-be. For them, pro-Palestinian leanings are as natural, as elegant, and as correct as the American Colony's famous Saturday-morning brunch.

The culture of the press is almost entirely Left. These are people who feel the weakness of democratic values, their own values; who enjoy the frisson of sidling up to a threatening civilization that coddles them even while holding in disdain the system they represent. Twice a day the muezzin calls from the minaret right outside the wall of the hotel. Sitting by the pool, one feels very near Ramallah, only a few kilometers away, where the children sent to the head of the demonstrations are throwing stones at Israeli soldiers their own age or slightly older. The children are fixed in one's consciousness in all their touching humanity, while the Jewish inhabitants of nearby Psagot, showered with bullets nightly by Arafat's Tanzim in Ramallah, seem but so many insensate obstacles on the road to peace and justice.

Besides, "settlers," like those in Psagot, by definition can never be "victims," just as the Israeli army by definition never responds to fire but rather actively shoots at child demonstrators. BBC or CNN broadcasts begin: "Israeli helicopters attacked Beit Jalla tonight." Only then will they add: "Just before, shots from houses in the Palestinian village hit the neighborhood of Gilo." In some reports it has become customary to call Gilo itself, where 45,000 Jews dodge bullets, a "settlement"—that is, another colonial intrusion, another obstacle to peace and justice.

In the shelter of the American Colony, meanwhile, Palestinian spokesmen repeat their familiar themes of victimization and triumph, deploying the moral high cards of freedom, justice, and self-determination. Who is to question them? Because they come from an authoritarian society, they themselves are magically imbued with authority. European or American journalists pose respectful questions to representatives of the Palestinian Authority (PA) and note down their answers quite as if it were possible to investigate these statements or to check them against alternative Palestinian sources at any time. Since it is not possible, the only thing that makes news in the end is the ever-climbing number of dead and wounded. And that too is impossible to verify.

Not even the world-famous episode of the little boy killed by cross-fire in Gaza, whose death, captured on film, was aired ceaselessly to demonstrate the barbarity of the Jews, was subject to investigation by the world press. Although the Israeli army ultimately determined that the fatal bullet may well have originated not from the Israeli checkpoint but from one of the seven locations from which *Palestinians* were shooting, this could hardly be expected to gain traction against the idea that the child was a martyr, a *shahid*, murdered by the Jews. From the very beginning, the exact cause of his death was never considered *worth* investigating, lest it impinge on the axiom that Israel was committing "aggression against unarmed people" and causing "the daily massacre of children."

The most flagrant instance of this syndrome in action involved the journalist Ricardo Cristiano from RAI, the Italian state television network. On October 12, two Israeli reservists on their way through Ramallah were seized, beaten, lynched, and horrifically mutilated at the hands of Palestinian police and a civilian mob. PA forces on the scene promptly hunted down and confiscated film and videotape of the incident to prevent its being aired—but not before a crew from a private Italian TV channel managed to send a clip of the atrocity to Rome that was soon broadcast around the world. Thereupon Cristiano published a letter of apology in the official Palestinian daily, *Al-Hayat Al-Jadida.* In it, he explained that he and RAI were not the ones at fault; blamed the misdeed on his colleagues at Mediaset, owned by Italy's right-wing opposition leader Silvio Berlusconi; reiterated his commitment to "respect" the "rules" laid down by the Palestinian Authority—rules that presumably prohibit anti-PA reporting; and promised to bend every effort to prevent similar images being shown in the future.

A more explicit statement of fealty, or a more outrageous violation of journalistic integrity, can scarcely be imagined. Yet, with one or two honorable exceptions, the reaction was muted both in Italy and elsewhere. Cristiano himself went back to Rome, and neither the directors of RAI nor its owners—that is, the Italian government—seemed to feel the need for further explanation. As for the community of journalists in Israel, at most they bestirred themselves to blame both the Palestinian Authority and the Israeli government for creating difficulties for the working press, with one Dutch correspondent taking the occasion to accuse the Israeli army, preposterously, of shooting at journalists.

But what else could be expected of a profession that does not even appear to know that it has struck a pact with Palestinian censorship? Every day, the "rules" that Cristiano declared he "respected" find a positive echo in the hearts of those who somehow cannot bring themselves to film, or to air, images of shooting by Tanzim or Palestinian police who have been positioned in the farther ranks of the demonstrating mobs, behind the stone-throwing children in the front rows. For such images would violate the tacit agreement by which Palestinians are to be seen always as victims, Israelis always as aggressors.

· · · · ·

The stance of the media is, at bottom, simple. The reasons behind it, however, are complex. Not least among them, tragically, is the stance Israel takes toward itself. It is a country many of whose elites are insupportably suffused with a sense of guilt, lacerated by historical revisionism, starved for world sympathy, scarred by too many wars. Nowhere are the wounds more visible than in Israel's own press.

Just recently, the weekend insert of *Ha'aretz*, the country's equivalent of the *New York Times*, featured three main articles. The first, replete with a devastating caricature, focused on Ehud Ya'ari, a veteran television commentator who specializes in diplomatic and military matters and who happens to be less than enamored of Yasir Arafat; in it, this generally sensible and well-informed observer was accused of harboring a pathological antipathy that invalidated his right to speak as a professional commentator on Palestinian affairs. The second article was devoted to interviews with Palestinian mothers; but instead of asking why they send their underage children out to die—or at least why they do not prevent them from going—the author drew from their testimony of selfless dedication a profound and heartrending lesson that Israeli women in particular needed to heed. In the third, pilots who had taken part in helicopter attacks on Palestinian police headquarters after the lynching of the Israeli soldiers in Ramallah were invited to share their feelings; they duly voiced their remorse over any civilian casualties that might have occurred. (Like most citizens of advanced democratic countries, Israelis have a real horror of war and of killing in war.)

Even the army seems to lack the conviction to justify itself, thus reinforcing the impression that Israel is in the wrong and on the defensive. At a press briefing, one high-level general ruled out the possibility that anything could be done effectively to deter Arab aggression. The problem, he said, was technical: Palestinian civilians have been mixed in with riflemen, and so far the army has been at a loss to deal with this particular battle tactic. Not once did he state for the benefit of the assembled newsmen that (quite apart from such practical questions) Israel has an absolute right to protect itself against violence directed at its citizens and soldiers. By contrast, Palestinian spokesmen like Hanan Ashrawi or Ziad Abu Zayyad or Saeb Erekat never miss an opportunity to begin their story from the top: this is our land, and ours alone, and the Jews who are occupying it are employing armed force against an unarmed people.

This, incidentally, may help explain, though it hardly excuses, the press's growing habit of viewing all of Israel as contested territory, not to mention its total lack of interest in Israel's painful and ultimately useless efforts over the last years to make territorial concessions to Arafat and the PLO. That, for example, in the latest negotiations at Camp David, Barak offered 92 percent of the West Bank, a sizable portion of Jerusalem, and a formula for international control of the Temple Mount seems to have done little to change the impression that Israel's "occupation" of age-old Arab lands is not a contingent fact rooted in particular historical circumstances but an innate character trait of the Jewish state, which *in its entirety* sits on "conquered Palestinian territory."

Occluded in this version of history, history as seen from the American Colony hotel, is the reality that Jerusalem is the established capital of the state of Israel, and that Hebrew, not Arabic or English, is the prevailing tongue in its streets. Only "in Jewish tradition," as Palestinian spokesmen like to put it, meaning in the imagination of the Jews, is the Temple Mount the site where the First and Second Temples stood. By such creeping semantic falsities, exactly as in the textbooks studied by Palestinian children, does the historical legitimacy of the Jewish presence in Jerusalem and Israel become, itself, a matter of contention.

It is difficult to believe that Israel's efforts to defend its actions before world opinion—necessary as such efforts are, weak and apologetic as they have been—can change matters in this respect, at least not in the short term. It is not just that we are talking about a profession, the world press, that is almost entirely uniform in its attitudes. The truth is that Israel, as the Jewish state, is also the object of a contemporary form of anti-Semitism that is no less real for being masked or even unconscious. (Arab Holocaust-denial, more violent and vulgar than anything in the West, is rarely if ever touched on in the mainstream media.)

And there is something else as well: looking into the heart of Arab regimes, preeminently including that of the Palestinians themselves, is simply too disturbing. For what one is liable to find there are disproportionate measures of religious and/or political fanaticism, bullying, corruption, lies, manipulation, and a carefully nurtured cult of victimhood that rationalizes every cruelty. On the streets and at the checkpoints, among the ardent, stone-throwing youths facing the armed might of the Israeli "aggressor," it is possible for a newsman to forget such discordant realities; at the American Colony, it goes without saying, they are never allowed to intrude.

—*January 2001*

Efraim Karsh

On the
"Right of Return"

B y the early 1990s, most Israelis, on both sides of the political spectrum, had come to embrace a two-state solution to their decades-long conflict with the Palestinian Arabs, a solution based on the idea of trading "land for peace." For these Israelis, and especially for the doves among them, the twilight hours of Ehud Barak's short-lived government came as a terrible shock.

During a span of six months, from the Camp David summit of July 2000 to the Taba talks a few days before his crushing electoral defeat in February 2001, Barak crossed every single territorial "red line" upheld by previous Israeli governments in his frenzied quest for an agreement with the Palestinians based on the formula of land for peace. Unquestioningly accepting the Arab side's interpretation of UN Security Council Resolution 242, passed in the aftermath of the Six-Day war of 1967, Barak's government offered to cede virtually the entire West Bank and Gaza Strip to the nascent Palestinian state, and made breathtaking concessions over Israel's capital city of Jerusalem. But to its amazement, rather than reciprocating this sweepingly comprehensive offer of land with a similarly generous offer of peace, the Palestinians responded with wholesale violence.

At Taba, the Palestinians also insisted, with renewed adamancy, on another non-negotiable condition that had been lying somewhat dormant in the background of the Oslo process begun in 1993. No peace would be possible, they declared, unless Israel guaranteed the right of the Arab refugees of the 1948–49 war, and their descendants, to return to territory that is now part of the state of Israel, and to be compensated financially for lost property and for decades of privation and suffering.

The reintroduction of this issue, at a moment when Israel had effectively agreed to withdraw to its pre-1967 lines, shook the Israeli peace camp to the core. All of a sudden, it seemed that the Arab states and the Palestinians really meant what they had been saying for so long—namely, that peace was not a matter of adjusting borders and territory but was rather a euphemism for eliminating the Jewish state altogether, in this case through demographic subversion. "Implementing the 'right of return' means eradicating Israel," lamented Amos Oz, the renowned author and peace advocate. "It will make the Jewish people a minor ethnic group at the mercy of Muslims, a 'protected minority,' just as fundamentalist Islam would have it."

Oz's plaintive cry struck no responsive chord with his Palestinian counterparts, however. "We as Palestinians do not view our job to safeguard Zionism. It is our job to safeguard our rights," stated the prominent politician Hanan Ashrawi, vowing to uphold the "right of return" even at the cost of undermining Israel's demographic balance. "The refugee problem," she continued, "has to be solved in total as a central issue of solving the Palestinian question based on the implementation of international law"; for not only has this right of return "never been relinquished or in any way modified," it "has been affirmed annually by the UN member states."

As it happens, Hanan Ashrawi is very much mistaken; and so, in his own way, is Amos Oz. There is no such collective "right of return" to be "implemented." But to grasp what is at issue here requires a deeper look into history, demography, international law, and politics.

II

Whatever the strengths and weaknesses of the Palestinians' legal case, their foremost argument for a "right of return" has always rested on a claim of unprovoked victimhood. In the Palestinians' account, they were and remain the hapless targets of a Zionist grand design to dispossess them from their land, a historical wrong for which they are entitled to redress. In the words of Mahmoud Abbas (a/k/a Abu Mazen), Yasir Arafat's second-in-command and a chief architect of the 1993 Oslo accords: "When we talk about the right of return, we talk about the return of refugees to Israel, because Israel was the one who deported them." The political activist Salman Abu Sitta has put it in even more implacable terms:

There is nothing like it in modern history. A foreign minority attacking the national majority in its own homeland, expelling virtually all of its population, obliterating its physical and cultural landmarks, planning and supporting this unholy enterprise from abroad, and claiming that this hideous crime is a divine intervention and victory for civilization. This is the largest ethnic-cleansing operation in modern history.

One may be forgiven for pausing a moment at the last sentence. To identify the Palestinian exodus—some 600,000 persons at most—as "the largest ethnic-cleansing operation in modern history" requires at the very least a drastic downgrading of other rather well-documented incidents: the 15 million ethnic Germans forced out of their homes in Eastern Europe after World War II; the millions of Muslims and Hindus fleeing the newly established states of India and Pakistan during the partition of the Indian subcontinent in 1948; the millions of Armenians, Greeks, Turks, Finns, Bulgarians, and Kurds, among others, driven from their lands and resettled elsewhere during the 20th century; and so forth and so on.

But put aside the hyperbole. The claim of premeditated dispossession is itself not only baseless, but the inverse of the truth. Far from being the hapless victims of a predatory Zionist assault, the Palestinians were themselves the aggressors in the 1948–49 war, and it was they who attempted, albeit unsuccessfully, to "cleanse" a neighboring ethnic community. Had the Palestinians and the Arab world accepted the United Nations resolution of November 29, 1947, calling for the establishment of two states in Palestine, and not sought to subvert it by force of arms, there would have been no refugee problem in the first place.

It is no coincidence that neither Arab propagandists nor Israeli "new historians" have ever produced any evidence of a Zionist master plan to expel the Palestinians during the 1948 war. For such a plan never existed. In accepting the UN partition resolution, the Jewish leadership in Palestine acquiesced in the principle of a two-state solution, and all subsequent deliberations were based on the assumption that Palestine's Arabs would remain as equal citizens in the Jewish state that would arise with the termination of the British Mandate. As David Ben-Gurion, soon to become Israel's first prime minister, told the leadership of his Labor (Mapai) party on December 3, 1947: "In our state there will be non-Jews as well—and all of them will be equal citizens; equal in everything without any exception; that is: the state will be their state as well."

In line with this conception, committees laying the groundwork for the nascent Jewish state discussed in detail the establishment of an Arabic-language press, the improvement of health in the Arab sector, the incorporation of Arab officials in the government, the integration of Arabs within the police and the ministry of education, and Arab-Jewish cultural and intellectual interaction. No less importantly, the military plan of the Hagana (the foremost Jewish underground organization in mandatory Palestine) for rebuffing an anticipated pan-Arab invasion was itself predicated, in the explicit instructions of Israel Galilee, the Hagana's commander-in-chief, on the "acknowledgement of the full rights, needs, and freedom of the Arabs in the Hebrew state without any discrimination, and a desire for coexistence on the basis of mutual freedom and dignity."

The Arabs, however, remained unimpressed by Jewish protestations of peace and comity. A few days before the passing of the UN partition resolution, Hajj Amin al-Husseini, the former mufti of Jerusalem and then head of the Arab Higher Committee (AHC), told an Egyptian newspaper that "we would rather die than accept minority rights" in a prospective Jewish state. The secretary-general of the Arab League, Abd al-Rahman Azzam, promised to "defend Palestine no matter how strong the opposition." "You will achieve nothing with talk of compromise or peace," he told a secret delegation of peace-seeking Zionists in September 1947:

> For us there is only one test, the test of strength.... We will try to rout you. I am not sure we will succeed, but we will try. We succeeded in expelling the Crusaders, but lost Spain and Persia, and may lose Palestine. But it is too late for a peaceable solution.

· · · · ·

In the event, the threats to abort the birth of Israel by violence heralded the Palestinians' collective undoing. Even before the outbreak of hostilities, many of them had already fled their homes. Still larger numbers left before war reached their doorstep. By April 1948, a month before Israel's declaration of independence, and at a time when the Arabs appeared to be winning the war, some 100,000 Palestinians, mostly from the main urban centers of Jaffa, Haifa, and Jerusalem, and from villages in the coastal plain, had gone. Within another month those numbers had nearly doubled; and by early June, according to an internal Hagana report, some 390,000 Palestinians had left. By the time the war was over in 1949, the number of refugees had risen to between 550,000 and 600,000.

Why did such vast numbers of Palestinians take to the road? There were the obvious reasons commonly associated with war: fear, disorientation, economic privation. But to these must be added the local

Palestinians' disillusionment with their own leadership, the role taken by that leadership in forcing widespread evacuations, and, perhaps above all, a lack of communal cohesion or of a willingness, especially at the highest levels, to subordinate personal interest to the general good.

On this last point, a number of Palestinians have themselves spoken eloquently. "There was a Belgian ship," recalls Ibrahim Abu Lughod, an academic who fled Jaffa in 1948,

> and one of the sailors, a young man, looked at us—and the ship was full of people from Jaffa, some of us were young adults—and he said: "why don't you stay and fight?" I have never forgotten his face, and I have never had one good answer for him.

Another former resident of Jaffa was the renowned Palestinian intellectual Hisham Sharabi, who in December 1947 left for the United States. Three decades later he asked himself "how we could leave our country when a war was raging and the Jews were gearing themselves to devour Palestine." His answer:

> There were others to fight on our behalf; those who had fought in the 1936 revolt and who would do the fighting in the future. They were peasants ... [whose] natural place was here, on this land. As for us—the educated ones—we were on a different plane. We were struggling on the intellectual front.

In fact, the Palestinian peasants proved no more attached to the land than the educated classes. Rather than stay behind and fight, they followed in the footsteps of their urban brothers and took to the road from the first moments of the hostilities. Still, the lion's share of culpability for the Palestinian collapse and dispersion does undoubtedly lie with the "educated ones," whose lack of national sentiments, so starkly portrayed by Sharabi and Abu Lughod, set in train the entire Palestinian exodus.

In 1948, both the Jewish and the Arab communities in Palestine were thrown into a whirlpool of hardship, dislocation, and all-out war—conditions that no society can survive without the absolute commitment of its most vital elites. Yet while the Jewish community (or Yishuv), a cohesive national movement, managed to weather the storm by extreme effort, the atomized Palestinian community, lacking an equivalent sense of corporate identity, fragmented into small pieces. The moment its leading members chose to place their own safety ahead of all other considerations, the exodus became a foregone conclusion.

The British High Commissioner for Palestine, General Sir Alan

Cunningham, summarized what was happening with quintessential British understatement:

> The collapsing Arab morale in Palestine is in some measure due to the increasing tendency of those who should be leading them to leave the country.... In all parts of the country the effendi class has been evacuating in large numbers over a considerable period and the tempo is increasing.

Hussein Khalidi, Secretary of the Arab Higher Committee, was more forthright. "In 1936 there were 60,000 [British] troops and [the Arabs] did not fear," he complained to the mufti on January 2, 1948. "Now we deal with 30,000 Jews and [the Arabs] are trembling in fear." Ten days later, he was even more scathing. "Forty days after the declaration of a *jihad*, and I am shattered," he complained to a fellow Palestinian. "Everyone has left me. Six [AHC members] are in Cairo, two are in Damascus—I won't be able to hold on much longer.... Everyone is leaving. Everyone who has a check or some money—off he goes to Egypt, to Lebanon, to Damascus."

The desertion of the elites had a stampede effect on the middle classes and the peasantry. But huge numbers of Palestinians were also *driven* out of their homes by their own leaders and/or by Arab military forces, whether out of military considerations or, more actively, to prevent them from becoming citizens of the Jewish state. In the largest and best-known example of such a forced exodus, tens of thousands of Arabs were ordered or bullied into leaving the city of Haifa against their wishes and almost certainly on the instructions of the Arab Higher Committee, despite sustained Jewish efforts to convince them to stay.* Only days earlier, thousands of Arabs in Tiberias had been similarly forced out by their own leaders. In Jaffa, the largest Arab community of mandatory Palestine, the municipality organized the transfer of thousands of residents by land and sea, while in the town of Beisan, in the Jordan valley, the women and children were ordered out as the Arab Legion dug in. And then there were the tens of thousands of rural villagers who were likewise forced out of their homes by order of the AHC, local Arab militias, or the armies of the Arab states.

None of this is to deny that Israeli forces did on occasion expel Palestinians. But this occurred not within the framework of a premeditated

---

*I have recounted the Haifa story at some length in "Were the Palestinians Expelled?" *Commentary*, July–August 2000.

plan but in the heat of battle, and was dictated predominantly by ad-hoc military considerations (notably the need to deny strategic sites to the enemy if there were no available Jewish forces to hold them). Even the largest of these expulsions—during the battle over the town of Lydda in July 1948—emanated from a string of unexpected developments on the ground and was in no way foreseen in military plans for the capture of the town. Finally, whatever the extent of the Israeli expulsions, they accounted for only a small fraction of the total exodus.

It is true that neither the Arab Higher Committee nor the Arab states envisaged a Palestinian dispersion of this extent, and that both sought to contain it once it began snowballing. But it is no less true that they acted in a way that condemned hundreds of thousands of Palestinians to exile. In early March 1948, the AHC issued a circular castigating the flight out of the country as a blemish on both "the *jihad* movement and the reputation of the Palestinians," and stating that "in places of great danger, women, children, and the elderly should be moved to safer areas" within Palestine. But only a week later, the AHC was evidently allowing those same categories of persons to leave Jerusalem for Lebanon, and also ordering the removal of women and children from Haifa. By late April, nothing remained of the AHC's stillborn instruction as Trans-Jordan threw its doors open to the mass arrival of Palestinian women and children and the Arab Legion was given a free hand to carry out population transfers at its discretion.

• • • • •

Muhammad Nimr al-Khatib, a prominent Palestinian leader during the 1948 war, summed up his nation's dispersion in these words: "The Palestinians had neighboring Arab states which opened their borders and doors to the refugees, while the Jews had no alternative but to triumph or to die."

That is true as far as it goes—yet it severely underplays the extent of mutual recrimination between the Palestinians and their supposed saviors. From the moment of their arrival in the "neighboring Arab states which opened their borders and doors," tension between the refugees and the host societies ran high. The former considered the states derelict for having issued wild promises of military support on which they never made good. The latter regarded the Palestinians as a cowardly lot who had shamefully deserted their homeland while expecting others to fight for them.

This mutual animosity was also manifest within Palestine itself, where the pan-Arab volunteer force that entered the country in early 1948 found itself at loggerheads with the community it was supposed to defend. Denunciations and violent clashes were common, with the local population often refusing to provide the Arab Liberation Army with the basic necessities for daily upkeep and military operations, and army personnel abusing their Palestinian hosts, of whom they were openly contemptuous. When an Iraqi officer in Jerusalem was asked to explain his persistent refusal to greet the local populace, he angrily retorted that "one doesn't greet these dodging dogs, whose cowardice causes poor Iraqis to die."

The Palestinians did not hesitate to reply in kind. In an interview with the London *Telegraph* in August 1948, the Palestinian leader Emile Ghoury blamed not Israel but the Arab states for the creation of the refugee problem; so did the organizers of protest demonstrations that took place in many West Bank towns on the first anniversary of Israel's establishment. During a fact-finding mission to Gaza in June 1949, Sir John Troutbeck, head of the British Middle East office in Cairo and no friend to Israel or the Jews, was surprised to discover that while the refugees

> express no bitterness against the Jews (or for that matter against the Americans or ourselves) they speak with the utmost bitterness of the Egyptians and other Arab states. "We know who our enemies are," they will say, and they are referring to their Arab brothers who, they declare, persuaded them unnecessarily to leave their home. . . . I even heard it said that many of the refugees would give a welcome to the Israelis if they were to come in and take the district over.

The prevailing conviction among Palestinians that they had been, and remained, the victims of their fellow Arabs rather than of Israeli aggression was grounded not only in experience but in the larger facts of inter-Arab politics. Indeed, had the Jewish state lost the war, its territory would not have been handed over to the Palestinians but rather divided among the invading forces, for the simple reason that none of the Arab regimes viewed the Palestinians as a distinct nation. Perhaps the clearest sign of this was that neither Egypt nor Jordan allowed Palestinian self-determination in the parts of Palestine they conquered during the 1948 war: respectively, Gaza and the West Bank. As the American academic Philip Hitti put the Arab view to a joint British and American committee of inquiry in 1946: "There is no such thing as Palestine in history, absolutely not."

So much for "the largest ethnic-cleansing operation in modern history."

III

But the appeal to history—to what did or did not happen in 1948–49—is only one arrow in the Palestinian quiver. Another is the appeal to international law, and in particular to the United Nations resolution that, as Hanan Ashrawi sternly reminds us, "has been affirmed annually by the UN member states."

The resolution in question, number 194, was passed by the UN General Assembly on December 11, 1948, in the midst of the Arab-Israeli war. The first thing to be noted about it is that, like all General Assembly resolutions (and unlike Security Council resolutions), it is an expression of sentiment and carries no binding force whatsoever. The second thing to be noted is that its primary purpose was not to address the refugee problem but rather to create a "conciliation commission" aimed at facilitating a comprehensive peace between Israel and its Arab neighbors. Only one of its fifteen paragraphs alludes to refugees in general—*not* "Arab refugees"—in language that could as readily apply to the hundreds of thousands of Jews who were then being driven from the Arab states in revenge for the situation in Palestine.

This interpretation is not merely fanciful. The resolution expressly stipulates that compensation for the property of those refugees choosing *not* to return "should be made good by the governments or the authorities responsible." Had the provision applied only to Palestinians, Israel would surely have been singled out as the compensating party; instead, the wording clearly indicates that Arab states were likewise seen as potential compensators of refugees created by them.

Most importantly, far from recommending the return of the Palestinian refugees as the only viable solution, Resolution 194 put this particular option on a par with resettlement elsewhere. It advocated, in its own words, that "the refugees wishing to return to their homes and live at peace with their neighbors should be permitted to do so at the earliest practicable date," but also that efforts should be made to facilitate the "resettlement and economic and social rehabilitation of the refugees."

It was, indeed, just these clauses in Resolution 194 that, at the time, made it anathema to the Arabs, who opposed it vehemently and voted unanimously against it. Linking resolution of the refugee issue to the achievement of a comprehensive Arab-Israeli peace; placing on the Arab states some of the burden for resolving it; equating return and resettlement as possible solutions, and diluting any preference for the former by means of the vague phrase, "at the earliest practicable date"; and above all establishing no absolute "right of return," the measure was seen, correctly, as rather less than useful to Arab purposes.

Only in the late 1960s, and with the connivance of their Soviet and third-world supporters, did the Arabs begin to transform Resolution 194 into the cornerstone of an utterly spurious legal claim to a "right of return," buttressing it with thinly argued and easily refutable appeals to other international covenants on the treatment of refugees and displaced persons. Today, after decades of fervent Palestinian rejection of the very idea of living "at peace with their neighbors," the most that can be said of those who invoke the language of Resolution 194 is that they are being disingenuous—though stronger and more accurate words also come to mind.

IV

And the refugees themselves? As is well-known, they were kept in squalid camps for decades as a means of derogating Israel in the eyes of the West and arousing pan-Arab sentiments. And there large numbers of them have remained, with the conspicuous exception of those allowed to settle and take citizenship in Jordan.

At the end of the 1948–49 war, the Israeli government set the number of Palestinian refugees at 550,000–600,000; the research department of the British Foreign Office leaned toward the higher end of this estimate. But within a year, as large masses of people sought to benefit from the unprecedented influx of international funds to the area, some 914,000 alleged refugees had been registered with the UN Relief and Works Agency (UNRWA).

More than a half-century later, these exaggerated initial numbers have swollen still further: as of June 2000, according to UNRWA, the total had climbed close to three and three-quarters million. Of course, UNRWA itself admits that the statistics are inflated, since they "are based on information voluntarily supplied by refugees primarily for the purpose of obtaining access to Agency services." (The numbers also include close to a million-and-a-half Jordanian citizens.) But the PLO, for its part, has set a still higher figure of 5 million refugees, claiming that many have never registered with UNRWA.

Aside from demanding an unconditional right of return for these individuals, Palestinian spokesmen have calculated that justice will also require monetary "reparations" in the amount of roughly $500 billion—half for alleged material losses, and the rest for lost income, psychological trauma, and nonmaterial losses. To this figure would also be added the hundreds of billions to be claimed by the refugees' host countries (notably Lebanon, Syria, and Jordan) for services rendered, bringing the total to about $1 trillion.

Needless to say, Israel has challenged UNRWA's figures, not to speak of the PLO's; it has unofficially estimated the current number of refugees and their families at closer to 2 million. But even if the more restrictive Israeli figures were to be accepted, it is certainly true, just as Amos Oz darkly predicts, that the influx of these refugees into the Jewish state would irrevocably transform its demographic composition. At the moment, Jews constitute about 79 percent of Israel's 6-million-plus population, a figure that would rapidly dwindle to under 60 percent. Given the Palestinians' far higher birth rate, the implementation of a "right of return," even by the most conservative estimates, would be tantamount to Israel's destruction.

Not that this stark scenario should surprise anyone. As early as October 1949, the Egyptian politician Muhammad Salah al-Din, soon to become his country's foreign minister, wrote in the influential Egyptian daily *Al-Misri* that "in demanding the restoration of the refugees to Palestine, the Arabs intend that they shall return as the masters of the homeland and not as slaves. More specifically, they intend to annihilate the state of Israel."

In subsequent years, this frank understanding of what the "right of return" was all about would be reiterated by most Arab leaders, from Gamal Abdel Nasser, to Hafez al-Assad, to Yasir Arafat. Only during the 1990s did the PLO temporarily elide the issue as it concentrated on gaining control of the territories vacated by Israel as part of the Oslo peace process. Its Israeli interlocutors, for their part, chose to think of the "right of return" as a PLO bargaining chip, to be reserved for talks on a final-status settlement and then somehow disposed of symbolically or through a token gesture of good will (such as by conceding some degree of Israeli "practical"—but not "moral"—responsibility for the 1948–49 exodus).

Throughout the 1990s, successive academic study groups, made up of the most earnestly forthcoming Israelis and the most grudgingly tractable Palestinians, devoted themselves to formulating a compromise proposal on this issue. They all failed—a fact that should have raised a large warning flag, but did not, even though the reason for the failure was plain enough. For the "right of return" is, for the Palestinians, not a bargaining chip; it is the heart of the matter.

That is why, over the decades, other perfectly commendable Israeli gestures toward dealing with the plight of the refugees have consistently met with indifference or rebuff. In 1949, Israel offered to take back 100,000 Palestinian refugees; the Arab states refused. Nevertheless, some 50,000 refugees *have* returned over the decades under the terms of Israel's family-reunification program, and another 75,000 who were displaced from the

West Bank and Gaza in the 1967 war have also returned to those territories. As Alexander Safian of CAMERA has documented, 90,000 Palestinians have also been allowed to gain residence in territory controlled
by the Palestinian Authority since the beginning of the Oslo process.
Safian similarly points out that millions have been paid by Israel in settlement of individual claims of lost property—"despite the fact that not
a single penny of compensation has ever been paid to any of the more
than 500,000 Jewish refugees from Arab countries."

Indeed, if one were to insist on the applicability of international
law, here is one instance where it speaks unequivocally. In 1948–49, the
Palestinians and Arab states launched a war of aggression against the
Jewish community and the newly-proclaimed state of Israel, in the process
driving out from their territories hundreds of thousands of innocent Jews
and seizing their worldly goods. Ever since, these same aggressors have
been suing to be made whole for the consequences of their own failed
aggression. Imagine a defeated Nazi Germany demanding reparations
from Britain and the United States, or Iraq demanding compensation for
losses it suffered during the 1991 Gulf war. Both legally and morally, the
idea is grotesque.

But in the end none of this matters. What is at issue in the dispute
over the "right of return" is not practicality, not demography, not legal-
ity, and certainly not history. What is at issue is not even the refugees
themselves, shamefully left in homelessness and destitution, and nour-
ished on hatred and false dreams, while all over the world tens of millions of individuals in similar or much worse straits have been resettled
and have rebuilt their lives. What is at issue is quite simply the existence
of Israel—or rather, to put it in the more honest terms of Muhammed
Salah al-Din, the still vibrant hope among many Arabs and Palestinians
of annihilating that existence, if not by one means then by another.

Tactically, "we may win or lose," declared Faisal Husseini, the
"moderate" minister for Jerusalem affairs in Yasir Arafat's Palestinian
Authority, in late March of this year; "but our eyes will continue to aspire
to the strategic goal, namely, to Palestine from the [Jordan] river to the
[Mediterranean] sea"—that is, to a Palestine in place of an Israel. "Whatever we get now," he continued, "cannot make us forget this supreme
truth." Until this "supreme truth" is buried once and for all, no amount
of Israeli good will, partial compensation, or symbolic acceptance of
responsibility can hope to create anything but an appetite for more.

—May 2001

Mark Helprin   Afterword

What Israel
Must Do to Survive

With the September 11, 2001 attack on the United States, the calculus of events in the Middle East has been sharply altered, but the fundamentals remain the same. Even the Gulf war—which in response to provocation of a different nature produced, a decade ago, the extraordinary cooperation of the world's greater and lesser powers, the largest single military operation in history, and a brilliant and unambiguous tactical victory—did not change them.

In Iraq, Saddam Hussein still rules. In Israel, the second *intifada* has been more ferocious than the first. With regard to the Arab-Israeli conflict, American policy has consisted not of deliberate inaction, which might have forced both the Arab states and the Palestinians toward accommodation of Israel, but of frenetic activism, the major operational component of which has been implied or actual pressure on Israel to accommodate the Arabs. And, despite protestations to the contrary, terrorism has been tolerated, and therefore encouraged.

The price of this flaccid toleration of terrorism has been its appearance on American soil and its escalation beyond the proportions of a Pearl Harbor. As we continue to sift through the ruins, it is clear that a war on terrorism must necessarily endure longer than the Gulf war; but it is not clear that the United States will summon the power or resolution it devoted to fighting Saddam Hussein (even if it then forfeited the end game), something of which America is always capable if rightly led and inspired.

Seriously to pursue and obliterate the terrorist networks, to punish and deter the distant states that harbor them, and to liquidate in those states the nuclear, chemical, and biological weapons and their infra-structure that are the real and present danger to this country will require of Americans the sacrifice of wealth, habit, custom, and lives. Though the war against terrorism may develop according to its own logic and acquire the doggedness for which America is noted, it also may not—especially if the terrorists knowingly quiet themselves so as to empower the forces of inertia and of the Left to break the resolution, official and non-official, that America has managed thus far.

Even should it suffer a more catastrophic blow before it begins to move as it can, the United States will survive. Its sinews of power still are intact and when mobilized are without question irresistible. Israel, however, has no such margin. And therefore it must be prepared, in the context of its alliance with the United States, to think differently and operate independently.

Independence is necessitated not only by the difference in scale between the two countries. Already in the early days after September 11, it was evident that, in the difficult task ahead, the United States had chosen a course in which success would depend in part on the recruitment of Middle Eastern regimes threatened by Islamism—a thing quite delicate, which, from the American perspective, has meant demanding of Israel the same kind of self-abnegation America asked of it, and received, during the Gulf war, and the same kind America asked, and received, after Oslo. To the extent that Israel cannot afford to abnegate itself, it must be self-reliant; and it must, of course, be self-reliant in any case.

For a short time, Israel may in some respects enjoy more freedom of action, and it will undoubtedly receive more military support from the United States, although much will be expected of it in return. But just as the spectacular and simultaneous fall of the Soviet Union and American victory in the Gulf war did not alter Israel's security situation except for the worse, so the apparently new world after September 11 will not alleviate Israel's problems. Even as the threat to Israel recedes temporarily to the background, it remains; indeed, its recession may make for more danger if it becomes the cause of neglect.

· · · · ·

If the current *intifada* drags on, and in anticipation of the next, it is important to keep in mind that throughout what used to be called the civilized but is now merely the developed world, polite intellectual society has customarily displayed for the Palestinian "resistance" a greater defer-ential admiration even than it once reserved for the aggressive powers of Communism. As in the cold war, not weakness of mind but want of courage has allowed the Left to equate consistently unequal moral propositions; to surrender to the relentless pressure of the primitive, the delusional, and the aggrieved; and thus to mix its lot, sometimes coyly, sometimes not, with terrorists, Islamists, and other self-declared enemies of Western civilization.

Is it necessary to state that this admiration is misplaced? As admirable as sacrificial struggle may be in the abstract, it is not admirable to push with every ounce of one's being for a violent revolution and then call this "resistance." It is not admirable to initiate and sustain insurrection so as to present oneself as its victim. It is not admirable to encourage children to give their lives to the television cameras for the sake of embarrassing an enemy that does not in any way want to shoot them but finds them deliberately and provocatively placed among riflemen spewing deadly fire. It is not admirable to make war in a fashion so primitive that one cannot grasp the elemental distinction between armed combatants and women and children, infants even, whom one deliberately targets and over whose death one rejoices. It is not admirable to revel in the blood of one's enemies, as in the Palestinian murders of the lost Israeli reservists in Ramallah last year, and to drink it, literally, as in the case of Black September's 1971 assassination of the Jordanian prime minister in Cairo. Nor is it admirable to do such things in the name of a historical claim that affords no right or justification whatsoever to one's opponent and admits no fault whatsoever of one's own.

The judgment of history should be straightforward: the almost ten-year-old Oslo misadventure was born of misconception, delusion, conformity, and cowardice. But not even the most startling and obvious evidence may be enough to revise the common wisdom. And if the common wisdom holds, the Palestinians will have reason to continue their policy.

What is their policy? It is, like the boa constrictor, to apply continual pressure, always tightening when the prey thrashes. It is to gain broad sympathy in the hope that the West will abandon Israel and the Arabs will unite against it, stimulated by outrages Israel wishes to avoid and the Palestinians to provoke. Thus, quite apart from the events of September 11, the destiny of Israel has been passing through the hands of the peacemakers into the hands of the war fighters. And although many people recoil from such a fact to the point of denying it, it is a fact nonetheless, and in the words of Winston Churchill, a statesman far greater than any who have touched of late upon the question of Palestine, facts are better than dreams.

· · · · ·

Contrary to the wisdom of the safe and chattering classes, Israel does not enjoy an assured military advantage, which is why Yasir Arafat may yet hope that before his death he can provoke the cataclysm that will exploit and prove this. In October of 1973, what stood between the rapidly advancing Egyptian army in the Sinai and an Israel that had yet to mobilize was not so much Egyptian hesitancy or fear of overextension as the existence of Israel's young nuclear deterrent. Since then, four Islamic states have attempted to acquire nuclear weapons, one has succeeded, and another may have; American arms have swelled Arab arsenals; Israel's strategic depth has been reduced to almost nothing; its martial ethos has been drastically diminished; and the millions of Palestinians living within Israel's lines of defense have become intimate with the country of their enemy, have organized themselves, acquired weapons, and established an army. Whereas all this is not insuperable, and countervailing factors exist in Israel's favor, the threat is mortal nonetheless. And only by confronting it, rather than by chasing the illusion that Arab enmity has in any way been assuaged, will Israel find its salvation.

If Israel is to survive, it must prepare more assiduously than it has yet done for four types of warfare: political war on the world stage, civil war, conventional war, and a war of weapons of mass destruction. As much as it should try to avoid fighting without benefit of patronage or allies, it must be ready, *in extremis,* to do so. And despite its long exhaustion it has to prepare its defenses with the gravity of a people who once more in modern memory are facing the prospect of destruction.

· · · · ·

Political warfare first: the Barak years were few but seemed like a millennium, as the failings of previous governments were compressed into spasmodic tropisms of surrender. In view of the upshot—the latest *intifada* and the world's response—Israel will have to recalibrate its approach to international politics. In particular, it must be willing to give up even American support rather than put itself in an untenable position. That is simply because a truly untenable position offers no second chance. Given American pragmatism, Israel's honest and necessary refusal to place itself in jeopardy for the sake of genuine American interests will sometimes be worth the risk, and for the sake of merely wishful diplomatic initiatives will always be.

Just as Israel need not give way to utopian diplomacy, it also need not forever lose the war of opinion. Everything the Palestinians do, every action, statement, initiative, and act of terrorism, is an assertion of their fundamental argument of the Palestine question. The root of their power is that they live and breathe the elemental. Israel shirks from this as if its own arguments were weak or its survival assured, neither of which is true. It must learn once again to stand its ground and return argument for argument, not only because it unashamedly claims justice but because its survival is directly at stake. It must state with clarity not only that its right to existence is indisputable but that the Palestinians and their Arab allies have never been willing to compromise, have been consistently absolutist, have made war after war, embrace violence as their policy and express pride in their atrocities, have created more Jewish refugees than the Palestinian refugees whom they have created in large part as well, and speak one way among themselves and another way to the world.

Next, civil warfare: Israel's ill-advised incorporation of the Palestinians into its national life has already brought about a de facto civil war, one that has the potential to intensify in conjunction with an attack from without. Rare is the nation at war that must fight simultaneously on and within its frontiers, as Israel is obliged to do even when at "peace." In support of an external attack, Palestinians organized in Spetsnaz-like units could bring mass terror to Israel's cities, block its mobilization, box in its badly concentrated nuclear forces simply by obstructing the roads necessary to their deployment, and attack air bases, arsenals, and military targets crucial to command and control.

That Israel acquiesced in arming the Palestinians is beyond understanding. But it can counter the Palestinian army in its midst if it creates fortified blocking and surveillance points along the "green line" dividing pre– and post–June 1967 Israel, as well as a mechanized infantry reserve cracked into fittingly small and highly mobile formations, and a corps of new special-forces units. It will have to arm, organize, and train able-bodied civilians along the lines of English home defense during World War II. As difficult and costly as urban warfare may be, the advantage lies with the defender, and it is an advantage that can be multiplied many times over by sensible and meticulous preparation.

In this *intifada* as in the previous one in the late 1980s, the greatest asset of Palestinian forces has been Israeli reluctance to fire upon unarmed crowds. A real war will assuredly liberate among Israelis the combative energy many Palestinians believe has been lost, but there is no question that Palestinian forces active in the initial stages of an attack will degrade

Israel's powers of conventional war. That is all the more reason for Israel not to take them for granted.

Which brings us to the third type of warfare. Without doubt, the hope of Arab planners is to leverage their combined assets with the support of Palestinian raids to throw Israel sufficiently off-balance to wear it down in armored and aerial campaigns. After the peace accords with Egypt in 1978, the 120 miles of strategic depth that Israel had acquired in the Sinai ceased to exist. The defensive lines of the West Bank have also been breached as a Palestinian army has arisen within them in slow motion during the years of illusion.

Israel has not been neglectful of conventional war fighting, and its skills in aerial combat, for example, provide a great advantage over the forces potentially arrayed against it. But were the Arabs to coalesce in a military alliance as they have done three times in the last half-century, and were they to display unexpected competence and imagination as they did in 1973, it would be of no little moment that they can field roughly 2,000 combat aircraft, of which 600 are first-line and largely American, against Israel's roughly 800, of which 400 are first-line. This would be especially dangerous if the surge of fighters were supported by surface-to-air missiles and radar-directed guns as they were in 1973, and if an initial attack on Israeli bases and command and control, by irregulars or surface-to-surface missiles, had degraded Israel's qualitative advantages and its absolute numbers alike.

In answer to conventional-force imbalances and surprises, Israel will have to enhance its military capacity and enrich its formations with, for example, an additional 200 first-line fighters and more attack helicopters, artillery, and infantry stand-off weapons. Diversion of more GDP to defense could substantially augment Israel's powers—and because of its situation, every power in Israel's possession needs augmentation to the point of overkill. In the decade 1970–1980, Israel devoted an average of 29.5 percent of GDP to defense. Now, with a real per-capita GDP several times higher, and therefore commensurately greater discretion in expenditures, it devotes only 9 percent. This is imprudent and without justification. Although diligent preparation is not merely a matter of money, it is mainly a matter of money. Apart from the direct effect, the more unambiguously Israel can overshadow would-be assailants in conventional war, the less likely they will be to exploit opportunities to attack it.

· · · · ·

As relevant to Israel's security as are international politics, the new Palestinian army, and conventional forces, all these are not nearly as important as weapons of mass destruction. Israel's small size, high population density, and urban character make it exceedingly vulnerable to such weapons, and it is neither a coincidence nor in reaction to Israel's own nuclear capacity that Libya, Iraq, and possibly Iran have nuclear-weapons programs; that in varying degree Libya, Syria, Iraq, and Iran possess chemical and/or biological weapons; and that North Korea successfully tested ballistic missiles financed by Iran, which may have at least two former Soviet tactical nuclear warheads suitable for attachment to the missiles of which it has been the sugar daddy. Though the various production timetables are uncertain, "Islamic" bombs exist already in Pakistan, which, despite the recent infusion of American support, is not that many steps away from a fundamentalist upwelling that could Talibanize its government.

One need not be versed in the arcana of nuclear effects, blast damage, and chemical/biological wind plumes—one need merely look at the map—to see that a nuclear-armed enemy willing to weather Israeli retaliation could either destroy the country right off or combine a lesser attack with other actions to break its resistance. Nuclear deterrence depends upon rational actors. The murderous potentates and semipsychotic visionaries with whom the Middle East is amply stocked are not always interested in rational calculation. Like Hitler, the Mahdi, or the Boxers, they tend to believe in destiny or divine protection, and their role in history has always been to jump off the cliff inexplicably. As Hitler might have said, and Saddam Hussein might say today, "This is what I do."

What can Israel do? It can embark, first of all, upon a more intensive civil-defense program, on the model of Switzerland and Sweden; that it has not done so already is reprehensible. This means appropriate shelters, immunizations, stockpiling of antidotes, provision of protective clothing and air filtration, etc., as if for a siege.

Then there is missile defense, which is the equivalent for Israel of David's five smooth stones. As everything may ride on a few seconds of combat, one can only hope that Israel has exceeded itself in the development of this last line of protection. And the line that stands just *before* it demands not only the exact intelligence necessary for Israel to preempt the use of weapons of mass destruction, but the will to do so.

Lately there has been a dearth of preventive attacks against the region's facilities for nuclear, chemical, and biological weapons, perhaps because of American pressure or because, in the years that Bill Clinton ate, Israel forgot that facts are better than dreams. Is it not obvious that now is the time, when American and Israeli interests with regard to weapons of mass destruction plainly coincide, for Israel to destroy the laboratories, reactors, processing plants, and depots whence untold terror might arise? Precisely this kind of creative destruction should be America's first imperative, and Israel's as well. It should be Russia's, England's, and France's, too, and that of every civilized nation.

In forging a broad coalition to pursue its war against terrorism, the United States may be turned from this imperative, not only because it may be too daunting for mere politicians to contemplate but because it will obviously be rather difficult to enlist the aid of the Arabs in destroying the weapons that are abuilding throughout the Arab world. But if, for the sake of forging a coalition that does not want to be forged, the United States abandons the destruction of weapons that must be destroyed, perhaps Israel can help to shore up its courage. Such a thing seems perilous, and it is, but hardly more perilous than its alternative.

Contributors

David Bar-Illan, a frequent commentator on Israeli affairs, has been the editorial-page editor and chief editor of the *Jerusalem Post,* and served as director of communications in the government of Benjamin Netanyahu.

Yigal Carmon, a former colonel in Israeli intelligence, served Prime Ministers Yitzhak Shamir and Yitzhak Rabin as adviser on countering terrorism (1998–1993). He is the founder and president of MEMRI, the Middle East Media Research Institute.

Douglas J. Feith, an attorney in Washington, D.C., is now Undersecretary of Defense for policy in the Bush administration. He served in the Reagan administration as Deputy Assistant Secretary of Defense and as a Middle East specialist on the White House National Security Council staff.

Dore Gold, the author of *U.S. Military Strategy in the Middle East,* was Israel's ambassador to the United Nations in 1997–1999. He is now the president of the Jerusalem Center for Public Affairs.

Nadav Haetzni writes about Palestinian affairs and other political and military matters for *Maariv,* one of Israel's leading newspapers.

Hillel Halkin is an essayist and critic who writes from Israel for *Commentary* and other publications.

Mark Helprin, whose novels include *A Soldier of the Great War, Winter's Tale, Memoir from Antproof Case,* and *Refiner's Fire,* is a contributing editor of the *Wall Street Journal* and writes widely on military and strategic affairs.

Efraim Karsh, head of Mediterranean studies at King's College, University of London, is the author of *Fabricating Israeli History: The New Historians* and (with Inari Karsh) *Empires of the Sand: The Struggle for Mastery in the Middle East.*

Fiamma Nirenstein, an Italian journalist who writes from Israel for the daily *La Stampa* and the weekly *Panorama,* is the author of *Israel: Peace in War.*

Daniel Pipes is director of the Middle East Forum and the author of, among other books, *Conspiracy: How the Paranoid Style Flourishes, and Where It Comes From.*

Norman Podhoretz is editor-at-large of *Commentary,* a senior fellow at the Hudson Institute, and the author of eight books.

Yuval Steinitz is a senior lecturer in philosophy at Haifa University and the author of numerous articles on the Arab-Israeli conflict. Formerly an activist in the Peace Now movement, he now serves as a member of Israel's parliament (Knesset) for the Likud party.

Index